THE FINE ART
OF
DINING

This book is dedicated to the residents of
the Elizabeth FitzRoy Homes in celebration of
thirty-five years of caring for those with
profound learning disabilities.

THE FINE ART
OF
DINING

ILLUSTRATED BY GRAHAM RUST

WITH RECIPES FROM WORLD-FAMOUS
CHEFS AND KITCHENS

◆

COMPILED AND EDITED BY FIONA GORE LANGTON,
MADOLYN WILSON AND ROSEMARY CAREY

A Bulfinch Press Book
Little, Brown and Company
BOSTON · NEW YORK · TORONTO · LONDON

First Edition

ISBN 0-8212-2224-4
Library of Congress Catalog Card Number 95-75415
A CIP catalogue for this book is available
from the British Library

Designed by Andrew Barron and Collis Clements Associates

Published simultaneously in the United States of America
by Bulfinch Press, an imprint and trademark of
Little, Brown and Company (Inc.),
in Great Britain by Little, Brown and Company (UK) Limited
and in Canada by Little, Brown and Company (Canada) Limited

PRINTED AND BOUND IN ITALY

NOTES ON THE RECIPES
In the recipes three systems of measurement are given:
metric, imperial and US cups – in that order.
Cup measurements always refer to standard US cups
(which hold 240ml/8fl oz or 16 x 15ml tablespoons).
1 teaspoon equals 5ml, 1 tablespoon equals 15ml.
These correspond very closely to British and American
standard spoon measures but Australian readers should note
that their standard tablespoon contains 20ml.
The recipes in this collection have been adapted for the home kitchen
and some may differ slightly from similar restaurant presentations.

The editors and publisher have used their best endeavours
to ensure the accuracy of the biographies at the time of going to press,
and will be happy to incorporate any amendments in
subsequent editions.

ACKNOWLEDGEMENTS

On behalf of the Elizabeth FitzRoy Homes, we would like to express our heartfelt thanks to all those who have made this publication possible:

Graham Rust for his extremely generous donation of original artwork.

The chefs, restaurants and cooks who generously gave their time and expertise to ensure that this cookery book would be of the highest standard.

The Board of Booker Fitch plc for their outstanding support.

The Countess of Euston and The Lady Tanlaw for their foresight and encouragement.

Mrs R. Vincent Lynch and her committee for the long hours spent organizing and compiling the biographical information.

Elsie Burch Donald for her advice and direction.

Mrs Cecil Eppel for her kind help throughout.

And the following individuals for their enthusiastic participation and support – Mr and Mrs Robert Acworth, Mrs F. Allen, Mrs Mary Altoft, Les Ambassadeurs Members Club, Mrs Juliet Angelastri, Gladys Baidoo, Tracey Bailey, Gordon Barber, Tim Barnum, Benjamin Batsch, The Beefsteak Club, Miss Juliet E. Berkeley, The Hon. Mrs Lavinia Bolton, Mrs Stephen Bonner, François Borne, Autumn Bradley-Cole, Mrs Theodore Botts, Mrs Sylvia Brandram, Maria Brunskill, Steven Butler, Helen Campbell-Smith, Mrs Charlotte Carey, Elio Carson, Mrs Christopher Carter, Miss Sally Carter, Thomas Catherall, Mrs Victor Cazalet, The Chester Grosvenor Hotel, Mrs Charles Chevasco, Mrs Jose Grant Chrichton, Glynn Christian, The Churchill Hotel, Miss Maureen Clark, Mr and Mrs Andrew Clement, Mrs James Codrington, Mrs K.P. Collins, Mrs Anthony Cooper, Lady Alexandra Cotterell, Mrs P.D. Crabbe, Colin Cripps, Neri D'Almedia, the late Elizabeth David, Maria Di Dia, Mrs Peter Driscoll, Mrs Timothy Dudgeon, Mrs Kathy Duffy, Charlotte Duncombe, Simon James Eldridge, Mrs Gervase Elwes, Jonathan Elwes, Emeril's Restaurant, Mrs David Emmerson, Susan Epstein, Mrs A.J. Trustram Eve, Mrs Philip Ferrier, Lady Fieldhouse, Jonathan Franklin, Sarah Garland, Christopher Gatto, Michael Gilday, Mrs Lesley Gillick, Mrs Sheila Glorioso, Mrs Margaret Goodrich, Jenny Graham, Gravetye Manor, Alan Greaves, Mrs Lydia Hadjipateras, Ange Hall, Derek Hamlem, Mrs John Harrison, Hartwell House, Lady Sara Havelock-Allan, Mrs Anthony Heller, John Hickey, Hiders Restaurant, Mrs Richard Hill, Mrs Moyra Hornor, House on the Hill Bed and Breakfast, Emily Hsu, Mrs Clive Hunt, Edward Hynes, The Hon. Mrs Owen Inskip, Richard Jagoda, Joe's Stone Crab Restaurant, Morgan Stanley International, John Isabel, Mrs J. James, Mrs Tom Kearney, Mrs Joe Keighley, Mrs Charles King, Miss Lynne Kitsull, Mrs William Kniesel, Mrs D. Lanham, Miss Christine Klein, L'Ortolan, Launceston Place Restaurant, Mrs Robert Lindemann, Lady Cameron of Lochiel, Mrs Eugene Lockhart, Diane de Loes, Edwina MacBeth, Mrs Lorna MacLeod, Mrs Richard Manley, Madame C. Mann, Lady Le Marchant, Eric Marin, Mrs Julian Marsham, Lisa McMahon, Miss Ashley Sarah Meade, Antone Medeiros, The Countess of Mexborough, Miller Howe Hotel, Mrs Philip Monbiot, Georgina Montagu, Mrs Sheila Morrell, Miss Elizabeth Morrell, Miss Joyce Moss, Mrs Judi Mould, Janice Murfitt, Armando Neerman, Mr and Mrs Peter Neumayer, The New Cavendish Club, Mrs Richard Nissen, The Old Manor, Richard Oberlin, Julia Ooi, Tricia Owen, Miss Georgina Oxley, Mrs Jean Palin, The Pelham Hotel, Clare Pilkington, Mrs Simon Pilkington, The Pillar House, Jacquette Refer, Mrs Patrick Rogers, Mr and Mrs William E. Ross, Mr and Mrs Michel Rosting, Mrs Rudiger von Eisenhart Rothe, The Duke of Roxburghe, Mrs Anne Sanderson, The Lady Scott, Mrs Mark Sheldon, Mrs Francis Sitwell, Jane Sleeman, Jeff Smith, Mrs Julian Smith, The Duchess of Somerset, Michael Spicer, Mrs Richard Stanton, Baroness Linda von Stauffenberg, The Rt. Hon. Sir David Steel, MP, Stephanie's, Peter Stowell-Phillips, Mrs Rahim Tadj-Saadat, The Lord Tanlaw, Miss Janice Taylor, Mrs Basil Thomas, Thornbury Castle, Maggie Thornton, Michelle Turner, Mrs William J. Tyne, Amy Valeiras, Mrs Greville Vernon, Vin Sullivan Foods, Mrs R. Vincent, Suzanne K. Wakamoto, Mrs Nicholas Wallop, Peggy Walmsley, Tim Watkins, Weald & Downland Open Air Museum, Mrs Jeffrey Weingarten, Mrs Clare Wilkins, Mrs Stephen Wood, Carol Young, Mrs Nicole Weinberg.

Elizabeth FitzRoy, driven by the desire to provide proper homes for children with a profound mental handicap, opened her first Home in 1962. Today seventeen homes are in operation across the country, providing homes for life to over two hundred residents. It is our hope to double in size by the year 2000.

Our goal is to assist in the development of each resident, to help them go forward and integrate as fully as possible into the community. An individually tailored program, utilizing the community and our own resources, is created for each and every resident. Today, there is a waiting list of hundreds of deserving individuals who urgently need a safe, productive home in which to live.

To answer this challenge, we need to raise £5 million by 1999, from the private sector, for the creation of new homes, facilities, equipment and the refurbishment of current properties.

We are deeply grateful to all those involved in the publication of this book for their efforts on our behalf.

Thirty years after Elizabeth FitzRoy opened her first home, the need to provide care for those with profound learning disabilities is as great as ever.

The most generous response of many contributors has resulted in this impressive and attractive cookery book, whose excellent presentation was guaranteed by the very special donation by Graham Rust of his own delightful illustrations. The proceeds will help sustain the more than two hundred individuals who are currently being cared for in the Homes, most of them for life.

As Patron, I hope that those who buy this book will enjoy the recipes, and I thank you most warmly for your support of the Elizabeth FitzRoy Homes.

Alexandra

CONTENTS

Soups
AND
Light Dishes

TARTARE OF MARINATED WILD SALMON WITH CUCUMBER SALAD

CONTRIBUTED BY CHEF RAYMOND BLANC
LE MANOIR AUX QUAT' SAISONS, GREAT MILTON, OXFORDSHIRE, ENGLAND

INGREDIENTS

450g/1lb fillet of wild salmon
1 Tbl chopped fresh dill
finely sliced zest of ⅛ lemon
1 Tbl caster/superfine sugar
1 Tbl salt
½ tsp Dijon mustard
2 tsp soured cream
1½ tsp fresh lemon juice
4 turns freshly ground white
   pepper

Continued opposite

Marinate the salmon:

1 Prepare the salmon by removing skin and tweezing out any stray bones.

2 In a large bowl, combine the dill, lemon zest, sugar and salt.

3 Place the salmon in the bowl – gently but thoroughly rub the mixture into it.

4 Wrap the salmon tightly in clingfilm – place in the bottom of the refrigerator for 12 hours (no longer).

5 At least 90 minutes before serving, unwrap the salmon, rinse under cold running water and pat dry.

6 In a bowl, combine the mustard, soured cream, lemon juice and white pepper.

7 Cut the salmon into 3mm/⅛in cubes, add to the bowl with the seasonings and mix thoroughly.

8 Taste and adjust seasonings – cover and refrigerate for 1 hour.

Serves 8

Equipment
clingfilm/plastic wrap
5–6cm/2–2½in plain pastry cutter

NOTES

Tartare de Saumon Sauvage à la Croque de Concombres (French)

Adapted from Recipes From Le Manoir Aux Quat' Saisons, Little, Brown, London.

Use only wild or the best farmed salmon for this dish. Marinate the fish for no more than 12 hours – after that time, wash and dry it, tightly wrap in clingfilm and keep refrigerated for up to 3 days until needed. Avoid cutting the salmon too finely (it will be like mince) or into too large pieces (it will be unattractive).

Prepare the cucumber salad:

1 Peel the cucumber and halve it lengthways. Using a teaspoon, scrape out the seeds.

2 Slice thinly, place in a colander and sprinkle with salt. Leave to sweat for 30 minutes (to remove indigestible acids).

3 Rinse under cold water and pat dry.

4 In a bowl, combine the vinegar, oil, salt and pepper. Add the cucumber slices, mix thoroughly and reserve.

Prepare the dish and serve:

1 Remove skin and pith from the lemon. Cut out the segments and slice them into wafer-thin triangles. Cover with clingfilm — reserve.

2 Cut off the tiny dill fronds, place in cold water and reserve — discard the stalks.

3 Place a pastry cutter in the centre of one of eight small plates. Fill nine-tenths full with salmon pieces, pressing down gently with the back of a spoon.

4 Top with 1 tsp soured cream. Smooth with a metal spatula.

5 Carefully lift off the pastry cutter and repeat with the remaining salmon.

6 Surround the salmon on each plate with a ring of overlapping cucumber slices.

7 Make a circle of lemon triangles on the top of the salmon and place a small mound of caviar in the centre of them.

8 Pat the dill dry on kitchen paper and arrange the tiny fronds like a royal garland around the top edge.

9 Serve chilled.

The cucumber salad can be prepared 2–3 hours in advance. The completed dish can be garnished and refrigerated up to 1 hour in advance (top with caviar immediately before serving to avoid any discoloration of the soured cream topping).

INGREDIENTS

For the cucumber salad
½ medium cucumber, plus salt for sprinkling
1 tsp white wine vinegar
2 Tbl non-scented oil
¼ tsp salt
2 turns freshly ground white pepper

To complete the dish
½ lemon
fresh dill
4 Tbl soured cream
1 Tbl caviar, salmon eggs or lumpfish roe — chilled

Serve with
brioche or hot, freshly prepared toast

FRESH PUMPKIN AND OYSTER SOUP

CONTRIBUTED BY CHEF WOLFGANG PUCK
WEST HOLLYWOOD, CALIFORNIA, USA

INGREDIENTS

1 pumpkin (2.7–3.6kg/6–8 lbs)
enough double/heavy cream to fill
   the pumpkin
1 tsp fresh thyme leaves
6 oysters
55g/2oz (½ cup) finely chopped
   celery
4 Tbl finely chopped shallots
120–240ml/4–8fl oz (½ to
   1 cup) dry white wine
cayenne pepper
fresh lemon juice
salt and freshly ground white
   pepper to taste

For the croûtons
2 Tbl clarified unsalted butter
6 × 1cm/½in thick slices of French
   bread – cut into small cubes

For the garnish
a sprinkling of chopped flat-leaf
   parsley

Prepare the croûtons:
1 In a frying pan, heat the clarified butter. Slowly sauté the bread cubes until lightly browned.
2 Remove, drain on kitchen paper and reserve.

Make the soup:
1 Preheat the oven to 190°C/375°F/Gas Mark 5.
2 Carefully remove the top of the pumpkin and take out the seeds.
3 In a saucepan, bring the cream to the boil. Pour into the pumpkin shell and add the thyme, and salt and pepper to taste.
4 Place the pumpkin on a small towel (to prevent it sliding or tipping) in a large baking tin and add 2cm/1in hot water. Bake for about 50 minutes, or until the flesh is soft, taking care not to puncture the shell when testing for doneness.
5 Meanwhile, in a covered saucepan, steam the oysters, celery and shallots in the wine just until the oysters open and render their juice. Retrieve the oysters from the shells and, if large, cut into 3 or 4 pieces – reserve. Through a muslin-lined sieve, strain the oyster juice into a bowl – reserve.
6 Pour the cream from the baked pumpkin into a large bowl.
7 Without puncturing the shell, scoop out the pumpkin flesh to leave a 1cm/½in-thick shell – add the flesh to the cream.
8 Add the reserved oyster juice to the cream. In batches, blend or process the mixture until smooth. Pour into a saucepan and bring to the boil. Reduce the heat to low and cook for 15–20 minutes to concentrate the flavours.
9 Season to taste with cayenne, lemon juice, salt and white pepper. Add the reserved oysters and allow them to heat in the soup for 30 seconds or so.
10 Place the pumpkin shell (firmly anchored on folded napkins or tea towels) on a platter. Fill the shell with the soup and garnish with fresh parsley. Place on the table, serving the croûtons on the side.

Serves 6

Equipment
large baking tin
muslin-lined sieve
food processor or blender

NOTES

Adapted from The Wolfgang Puck Cookbook, Random House, 1986.

This soup is served in the pumpkin, so choose an attractive one, and take care not to puncture or damage it during preparation.

CUCUMBER GAZPACHO

....

CONTRIBUTED BY VICTOR EDELSTEIN, LONDON

INGREDIENTS

2 large European/seedless
cucumbers – peeled and roughly
    chopped
½ loaf stale white bread
1 onion – chopped
3 Tbl olive oil
1 Tbl cider vinegar
150g/6fl oz/ (¾ cup) plain yoghurt
salt and freshly ground white
    pepper to taste
a sprinkling of fresh snipped chives
paprika

To garnish
1 tomato – peeled, seeded and
    chopped
hot, freshly made croûtons

1 Place the cucumber pieces in a bowl of salted water to soak for 30 minutes – drain.

2 Meanwhile, roughly tear out the inside of the bread loaf (reserve the crusts for making breadcrumbs) and place the pieces in a bowl. Cover with water and soak for 2–3 minutes. Remove the bread and gently squeeze out most of the water.

3 Place the cucumber, bread and onion in a blender or food processor – process to desired consistency. Pour the mixture into a bowl.

4 Add the olive oil, vinegar and yoghurt, and salt and pepper to taste. Refrigerate for 2 hours.

5 Sprinkle with fresh snipped chives and dust with paprika.

6 Serve in chilled bowls, with a side garnish of chopped tomato and hot croûtons.

Serves 6 to 8

Equipment
food processor or blender

NOTES

To make croûtons: in a frying pan heat 2 Tbl clarified butter. Cut a few slices of stale white bread into cubes of the preferred size, and slowly sauté until lightly browned. Remove, drain on kitchen paper and serve.

HOT AND SOUR PRAWN SOUP

CONTRIBUTED BY THE THAI COOKING SCHOOL
THE ORIENTAL HOTEL, BANGKOK, THAILAND

Prepare the spice paste:

1 Using a pestle and mortar, pound the spice paste ingredients together to a smooth consistency.

Make the soup:

1 In a large saucepan, bring half of the stock to the boil.

2 Add the spice paste – return to the boil, stirring well.

3 Add the galangal or ginger, lemongrass, prawns and remaining stock – return to the boil.

4 Season to taste with lime juice, fish sauce, shredded lime leaves and crushed chillies.

5 Serve immediately in heated bowls – garnished with fresh coriander leaves and strips of fresh chilli.

Serves 4

Equipment
pestle and mortar

NOTES

Tom Yaam Goong (Thai).

Greater galangal (khaa/laos/lenghuas) is a pungent rhizome generally preferred in Thai cuisine to the closely related fresh ginger. Fresh greater galangal is similar in appearance to knobby fresh ginger root but has a more delicate, pale cream to rosy skin, and protruding wood stalks. A mainstay of Thai cuisine, it is sold in oriental markets as fresh root, packaged dried slices and small containers of ground powder. Fresh ginger root makes an appropriate substitute with the optional addition of freshly ground black pepper and a few drops of lemon juice to adjust for galangal's more intensely spicy flavour.

Lemongrass, a fibrous aromatic grass related to the stronger scented citronella, is sold fresh in semi-dried stalks composed of tightly packed leaves. To use, cut off the dry top inch or so and peel away a few of the outer leaves to reveal the more tender core. Generally lemongrass is eaten very finely sliced or pounded into a paste, but in larger pieces it is used for flavouring and subsequently discarded. Dried lemongrass, available in some speciality markets, should be soaked in warm water for several hours before use. Lemon balm or several strips of lemon peel may be substituted but the taste is markedly different.

INGREDIENTS

For the spice paste
7 whole black peppercorns
1 Tbl finely chopped coriander/cilantro root (root and 7.5cm/3in of stems)

For the soup
1.2 litres/2 pints (5 cups) fish stock
3 slices greater galangal or fresh ginger
3 lemongrass stalks – finely sliced
370g/13oz medium uncooked prawns – shelled and deveined
4 Tbl fresh lime juice
4 Tbl fish sauce (nam pla or nuoc mam)
10 kaffir lime leaves – finely shredded
7 Thai chillies (prig khee nu) – crushed

To garnish
fresh coriander/cilantro leaves
fresh chilli – in fine strips

DARK MUSHROOM SOUP WITH PARMESAN TUILES

CONTRIBUTED BY HAMBLETON HALL, OAKHAM, LEICESTERSHIRE, ENGLAND

INGREDIENTS

1.4kg/3 lbs fairly large field
   mushrooms (opened out with
   dark gills)
1 Tbl non-scented oil
30g/1oz (2 Tbl) unsalted butter
1 onion – thinly sliced
1 clove garlic – roughly chopped
1 tsp chopped fresh thyme – or
   to taste
1 tsp chopped fresh rosemary –
   or to taste
scant 1 litre/1½ pints (3¾ cups)
   chicken stock
salt and freshly ground black
   pepper to taste

For the Parmesan tuiles
60g/2oz (½ cup) plain/all purpose
   flour
90g/3oz (½ cup) flaked/sliced
   skinned almonds
90g/3oz (¾ cup) freshly grated
   Parmesan cheese
45g/1½oz (3 Tbl) melted unsalted
   butter
1 egg white

Prepare the soup:

1 Clean the mushrooms thoroughly – trim and slice roughly.
2 In a large saucepan, heat the oil and butter.
3 Add the onion and garlic – cover and cook over low heat until soft and colourless.
4 Add the mushrooms and herbs – cover and cook over low heat until the mushrooms are soft and very dark.
5 Add stock – simmer for approximately 30 minutes.
6 Remove from heat – purée in a blender or food processor until smooth (if necessary, allow to cool uncovered – then cover and refrigerate until needed).

Make the Parmesan tuiles:

1 Preheat the oven to 200°C/400°F/Gas Mark 6.
2 In a large bowl, combine the ingredients to form a dough.
3 On a lightly floured surface, roll the dough out into a very thin sheet. Cut into 7.5cm/3in rounds and place on a greased baking tray. Bake for 8 minutes.
4 While still warm, form the tuiles into their characteristic curved shape by bending the rounds gently over a rolling pin, or rolling them up cigar fashion.

To serve:

1 Reheat the soup gently – season with a small amount of salt and freshly ground black pepper to enhance the flavour of the mushrooms.
2 Serve the soup in small heated soup cups with Parmesan tuiles on the side of each plate.

Serves 6

Equipment
food processor or blender
baking tray/sheet – greased

NOTES

This soup, while thick and dark in colour, contains no flour or cream.

Field mushrooms (Agaricus campestris) are members of the same family as cultivated mushrooms. A common type of wild mushroom, they grow in grassy expanses rather than around trees like many other wild species. In various shades of brown with wide caps and dark gills, they are widely available in UK markets but are largely unknown in the US, where open-capped cultivated mushrooms may be substituted.

ORIENTAL CHICKEN SOUP

CONTRIBUTED BY CHEFS FRANCES WARDE AND LUCY HILL
THE VANDERBILT RACQUET CLUB, LONDON

1 In a large saucepan, heat the oil.
2 Add the ginger and garlic — gently sauté until fragrant (don't let them brown).
3 Add the soy sauce, chilli sauce and stock.
4 Bring to the boil — lower the heat and simmer for 5 minutes.
5 Add the carrots and mushrooms, and salt and pepper to taste and simmer for 10 minutes.
6 Add the bean sprouts, spring onions and chicken. Bring to the boil.
7 Serve at once in heated soup bowls with a sprinkling of chopped coriander leaves.

Serves 6

INGREDIENTS

1 tsp groundnut/peanut oil
¼ tsp grated fresh ginger
1 clove garlic — finely chopped
2 Tbl light soy sauce
1 tsp oriental chilli sauce
1.2 litres/2 pints (5 cups) good
    chicken stock
120g/4oz (½ cup) carrots — finely
    sliced and cut into matchsticks
120g/4oz (1 cup) sliced button
    mushrooms
60g/2oz (1 cup) bean sprouts
1 bunch spring onions/scallions
    (both white and tender green
    parts) — cut into matchsticks
120g/4oz (1 cup) finely chopped
    cooked chicken
salt and freshly ground black
    pepper to taste

To garnish
chopped fresh coriander/cilantro
    leaves

Serve with
warm bread rolls

NOTES

This soup is not suitable for freezing.

Ginger root (fresh) is the pungent underground stem (rhizome) of the ginger plant and is sold in irregularly shaped "hands" in most food markets. Its fresh spicy taste goes particularly well with seafood and is essential to oriental cuisines. Look for firm, smooth "hands" which need not be peeled before use. Pickled ginger and dried ginger are also available in packets in oriental markets; neither is an appropriate substitute for fresh ginger, however.

Light soy sauce is the type commonly available in Western markets. There is also a dark soy sauce, which is stronger, available in oriental markets.

Oriental chilli sauce is a very spicy, bright red, slightly fruity sauce, often used as a condiment or dipping sauce. There are many brands available so experiment until you find one you particularly like. Do not confuse this with either chilli bean sauce (a much thicker, darker soybean-based cooking sauce) or chilli oil (an infusion of red peppers and oil).

SMOKED CHICKEN SALAD

CONTRIBUTED BY JEFFREY ARCHER, LONDON

Serves 4

1 Cut the chicken into strips — set aside.

2 Lightly salt the cucumber, leave to drain for 30 minutes, then rinse and pat dry — set aside.

3 Meanwhile, in a frying pan, heat the oil and fry the bacon until crisp. Remove, drain on kitchen paper and then crumble — set aside.

4 Add the bread to the pan of bacon oil. Fry until golden then remove and drain the croûtons on kitchen paper — set aside.

5 In a small saucepan, hardboil the quail eggs for 5 minutes. Shell and quarter them — set aside.

6 Wash and carefully dry the lettuce. Tear it into bite-size shreds and place in a salad bowl.

7 Add the spring onions, bean sprouts, mushrooms and raisins to the lettuce in the bowl and toss lightly. Put the chicken, cucumber, bacon, croûtons and quail eggs on top.

8 Peel, stone and chop the avocado and coat with the lemon juice. Add to the bowl.

9 In a separate bowl, make the dressing by whisking together all its ingredients.

10 Pour the dressing over the salad — fold it in carefully to avoid squashing the avocado or quail eggs. Serve immediately on brightly coloured salad plates garnished with cherry tomatoes and lightly sprinkled with snipped chives.

NOTES

Always dry salad greens thoroughly: water prevents the dressing from adhering to the leaves and can make a wonderful salad tasteless.

INGREDIENTS

450g/1lb skinned and boned smoked chicken
120g/4oz (1 cup) cucumber, peeled and chopped into chunks
2 tsp sunflower oil
120g/4oz (1/4 lb) streaky bacon
4 slices stale bread, in small cubes
6 quail eggs
225g/8oz (4 cups) best crisp lettuce in season
120g/4oz (1 cup) finely chopped spring onions/scallions
120g/4oz (2 cups) bean sprouts — washed and well drained
60g/2oz (½ cup) cleaned and quartered button mushrooms
30g/1oz (3 Tbl) raisins
1 avocado (ripe but not too soft)
2 Tbl fresh lemon juice

For the dressing
150g/5fl oz (¾ cup) plain yoghurt
2 Tbl mayonnaise
60g/2oz (½ cup) blue cheese — crumbled
salt and freshly ground black pepper to taste

To garnish
cherry tomatoes
a sprinkling of snipped fresh chives

Avocado Mousse and Tomato Salad

CONTRIBUTED BY CHEF MYRTLE ALLEN
BALLYMALOE HOUSE, COUNTY CORK, IRELAND

INGREDIENTS

For the dressing
I large clove garlic – crushed
60ml/2fl oz (¼ cup) white wine
   vinegar
180ml/6fl oz (¾ cup) olive oil
I tsp Dijon mustard
I spring onion/scallion – thinly
   sliced
I sprig fresh parsley
I level tsp salt and a few turns of
   freshly ground black pepper

For the mousse
½ tsp onion grated to a purée
3 tsp fresh lemon juice
120ml/4fl oz (½ cup) chicken stock
2 ripe avocados
10g/¼oz (I Tbl) gelatin powder
I Tbl warm water

For the tomato salad
6 tomatoes
½ tsp caster/superfine sugar
¼ tsp salt and a few turns of
   freshly ground black pepper
I rounded tsp chopped fresh
   herbs (any combination of basil,
   mint, thyme, tarragon)
I spring onion/scallion – thinly
   sliced

To garnish
fresh basil leaves

Prepare the dressing:
1 Put all the dressing ingredients into a food processor or blender and, at medium speed, reduce them to a smooth thick sauce – set aside.

Make the mousse:
1 In a bowl, combine the grated onion, lemon juice and stock with 120ml/4fl oz (½ cup) of the dressing.
2 Peel and stone the avocados. Place the flesh in the food processor or blender and purée, gradually adding the stock and dressing mixture.
3 In a heatproof bowl, soften the gelatin in the water – warm over a saucepan of boiling water until completely dissolved.
4 Thoroughly blend the gelatin into the avocado mixture.
5 Pour the mixture into the greased moulds and refrigerate until set (allow at least 6 hours).

Make the tomato salad and assemble the dish:
1 Peel and slice the tomatoes and sprinkle them with the sugar, salt and black pepper.
2 Immediately sprinkle the tomatoes with the fresh herbs, spring onion and just enough dressing to coat.
3 Arrange the tomato slices on each of four chilled serving plates, leaving room in the centre for the mousse.
4 Dip the moulds into a bath of hot water for a few seconds to loosen them. Turn out an avocado mousse on to each plate.
5 The dish may be kept chilled for up to 1 hour. Garnish with fresh basil leaves just before serving, and pass the remaining dressing on the side.

Serves 4

Equipment
food processor or blender
4 × 120ml/4fl oz (½ cup) oblong
   moulds – greased with
   sunflower oil

NOTES

Eat the mousse the day it is made to avoid any discoloration of the avocado.

Avocados are tropical fruits with rich buttery flesh. Choose ones that yield to gentle pressure without feeling "mushy". Two main types are on the market: Hass/California, the smaller of the two, with dark green "knobby" skin; and Fuerte/Florida, the larger, with smooth, bright green skin.

ROCKET SALAD WITH BOCCONCINI AND BASIL OIL

CONTRIBUTED BY CHEF DON PINTABONA, TRIBECA GRILL, NEW YORK CITY

INGREDIENTS

4 plum/roma tomatoes
I small red and I small yellow bell
    pepper
225g/8oz rocket/arugula – gently
    washed and thoroughly dried
    (trim any roots immediately
    before tossing)
15g/½oz (2 Tbl) pitted and
    chopped Niçoise olives
6 pieces bocconcini – sliced in half
5 Tbl tomato fondue (see facing
    page) – at room temperature
basil oil (see facing page)
tomato oil (see facing page)
salt and freshly ground black
    pepper

For the dressing
4 Tbl balsamic vinegar
salt and freshly ground black
    pepper to taste
4 Tbl virgin olive oil
2 Tbl roasted garlic oil (see facing
    page)

To garnish
fresh basil leaves

Oven-dry the tomatoes:
1 Preheat the oven to 100°C/200°F/Gas Mark 1.
2 Halve the tomatoes lengthways and arrange, cut-side up, on a baking tray/sheet. Sprinkle with salt.
3 Roast until enough moisture has evaporated to leave the tomatoes shrivelled and leathery but not scorched – this can take 4 to 6 hours; check every 45 minutes or so.
4 Chop the tomatoes.

Roast the peppers:
1 Char the skin by grilling or holding over an open flame until blistered and blackened evenly all over.
2 Enclose the peppers in a paper bag or tightly covered bowl for 20 minutes to allow the skin to steam away from the flesh.
3 When cool, remove seeds, ribs and skin with a paring knife. Cut the flesh into julienne strips.

Prepare the dressing:
1 In a bowl, whisk the vinegar with salt and pepper to taste until the salt is completely dissolved.
2 Whisking constantly, slowly add the olive and roasted garlic oils until the dressing is emulsified.

Assemble the salad:
1 In a large bowl, gently but thoroughly combine the oven-dried tomatoes, roasted peppers, rocket and olives with the dressing – season to taste.
2 Arrange the salad to make a "nest" in the centre of each of four chilled salad plates, using a mould if available.
3 Top each "nest" with 3 slices of bocconcini (press firmly into the salad but take care not to bruise the greens).
4 Garnish the plates with three evenly spaced heaps of tomato fondue along with small amounts of basil and tomato oils.
5 Season the bocconcini with pepper – garnish the salads with fresh basil leaves and serve immediately.

Serves 4

Equipment
plastic, circular mould – optional

NOTES

Bocconcini are small pieces of mozzarella cheese marinated in olive oil and a variety of herbs and spices – they are available in speciality stores.

To make tomato fondue:

1 In a heavy-bottomed saucepan, combine tomatoes with shallots and garlic (the proportions are to taste – remember all the flavours will concentrate).

2 Season with salt, pepper and any fresh herbs desired.

3 Cook very slowly for 2 to 3 hours until the mixture reduces to a light paste.

4 Store tightly sealed and refrigerated.

To make basil oil:

1 In a food processor or blender, purée the basil with the oil and the salt (this may have to be done in batches).

2 Pour into a tightly sealing bottle. Leave overnight before use.

To make tomato oil:

1 In a heavy-bottomed pan, sweat the garlic and shallots in a little of the olive oil for 10 to 15 minutes.

2 Add the fresh tomatoes and tomato purée and mix well.

3 Add the remaining olive oil and thyme and bring to the boil. Lower the heat and cook slowly for 20 minutes.

4 Remove from the heat and allow to cool.

5 Cover and allow to stand overnight in the refrigerator.

6 Strain – store tightly sealed and refrigerated.

To make roasted garlic oil:

1 Preheat the oven to 180°C/ 350°F/ Gas Mark 4.

2 Cut the garlic heads in half widthways – arrange, cut-side up, in a roasting pan and drizzle with a little of the olive oil. Add 2–3 Tbl of water to the pan, cover tightly and roast for 30 to 40 minutes.

3 Uncover the pan and continue roasting for 10 minutes longer.

4 Remove and allow to cool.

5 Gently squeeze the soft garlic pieces into a heavy-bottomed pan. Pour in the remaining olive oil and bring to the boil.

6 Store tightly sealed and refrigerated.

The fondue and the oils and be prepared in advance, stored in the refrigerator and used in other recipes of your choice or devising besides this one.

Oven-dried tomatoes can also stored: freeze them or preserve them in a tightly sealed jar covered with olive oil. Roasted peppers can be kept for later use if coated with olive oil and wrapped in clingfilm/plastic wrap.

INGREDIENTS

For tomato fondue
proportions to taste of the
  following:
tomatoes – peeled, seeded and
  chopped
shallots – finely chopped
garlic – finely chopped
salt, freshly ground black pepper
  and fresh herbs

For basil oil
5 bunches fresh basil
945ml/32fl oz (4 cups) olive oil
4 Tbl salt

For tomato oil
45g/1½oz (6 Tbl) sliced garlic
45g/1½oz (6 Tbl) sliced shallots
945ml/32fl oz (4 cups) olive oil
10 tomatoes – peeled, seeded
  and diced
6 Tbl tomato purée/paste
pinch of fresh thyme

For roasted garlic oil
5 whole garlic heads
945ml/32fl oz (4 cups) olive oil

PRICKLY PRAWNS

CONTRIBUTED BY CHEF MICHEL RICHARD
CITRUS, LOS ANGELES, USA

INGREDIENTS

For the purple sauce
6 Tbl mayonnaise
2 Tbl fresh lemon juice
1 Tbl red wine vinegar
1½ tsp light soy sauce
2 "thin coin" slices of fresh ginger
2 Tbl olive oil
340g/12oz (3 cups) finely sliced
    red cabbage
salt and freshly ground black
    pepper to taste

For the deep-fried prawns/shrimp
16 large uncooked prawns/shrimp
    – shelled and deveined
4 Tbl plain/all purpose flour
1 egg – at room temperature
1 Tbl water
salt and freshly ground black
    pepper to taste
170g/6oz (4 cups) kataifi
vegetable oil for deep-frying

To garnish
sprigs of fresh flat-leaf parsley or
    coriander/cilantro

Prepare the purple sauce:
1 In a food processor, combine the mayonnaise, lemon juice, vinegar, soy sauce and ginger – process until smooth.
2 With the processor on, gradually drizzle in the olive oil.
3 Add the sliced cabbage – process until coarsely chopped, scraping down the sides as necessary.
4 Season to taste, transfer to a bowl, cover and refrigerate if necessary. Bring to room temperature before serving.

Deep-fry the prawns:
1 Prepare 3 large shallow bowls for coating the prawns: 1 of flour; 1 of whisked egg and water seasoned with salt and pepper, and 1 of kataifi cut into 2.5cm/1in pieces (over the bowl) with threads gently separated.
2 Line a large baking tray with parchment paper.
3 One at a time, dip each prawn, first into the flour (until well coated) – pat off excess. Holding the prawn with tongs, coat it completely in egg mixture. Finally, dip into the kataifi then gently press in palm of hand to form a neat round shape.
4 Place the coated prawns on the lined baking tray.
5 Meanwhile, in a wok or large pan, heat 2.5cm/1in of oil to 180°C/350°F (or until bubbles form around a wooden chopstick or spoon handle immersed in the oil).
6 Using tongs, slowly dip 1 coated prawn into the hot oil, waiting until the bottom layer of kataifi sets before immersing completely (or the kataifi may pull away from the prawn).
7 Add additional prawns in the same manner (working in batches without crowding) and cook, turning several times, until golden-brown on both sides (about 3 minutes total). Drain cooked prawns on kitchen paper – keep warm.
8 As soon as the cooking is completed, arrange the prawns on warmed plates. Spoon the purple sauce into the centre, garnish with parsley or coriander and serve immediately.

Serves 8

Equipment
food processor
parchment paper
large baking tray/sheet
tongs

NOTES

Serves 4 as a main course.

Purple sauce may be prepared a day in advance and refrigerated.

Prawns can be prepared ahead of time on the day they are to be served, either breaded, covered and refrigerated before frying, or fried to be reheated in a 180°C/350°F/Gas Mark 4 oven for 2 to 3 minutes.

Kataifi is a popular shredded-wheat product that appears frequently in Middle Eastern cooking. Used in both savoury and sweet dishes, it is available packaged (like filo pastry) in most Eastern markets.

Native Oysters on a Bed of Leeks with Champagne Sauce

CONTRIBUTED BY CHEF PHILIP CORRICK
THE ROYAL AUTOMOBILE CLUB, LONDON

INGREDIENTS

24 native oysters
450g/1 lb leeks (white parts only)
  – trimmed
120g/4oz (8 Tbl) unsalted butter
30g/1oz (2 Tbl) finely chopped
  shallots
150ml/5fl oz (½ cup + 2 Tbl) dry
  champagne
150ml/5fl oz (½ cup + 2 Tbl) fish
  stock
300ml/10fl oz (1¼ cups)
  double/heavy cream
1 egg yolk, beaten
salt and freshly ground white
  pepper to taste

To garnish
sprigs of fresh chervil
sevruga caviar – optional

Serve with
warm rolls

1 Preheat the grill.

2 Scrub the outside of the oysters under cold water and open them, taking care not to damage the flesh (your fishmonger will do this but oysters must be used within a few hours of opening).

3 Place the oysters in a bowl. (Be on the lookout for any odd bits of oyster shell that might find their way into your sauce.) Reserve the deeper halves of the oyster shells, discarding the shallower halves.

4 Cut the leeks in half lengthways and wash under cold running water, fanning them open to be sure that all specks of dirt are washed out.

5 Cut the leeks into thin "julienne" strips. Blanch for 1 minute in boiling water, immediately refresh in cold water and drain thoroughly.

6 In a large, heavy-bottomed pan, heat 90g/3oz (6 Tbl) of the butter. Add the shallots, cover and cook over low heat until soft but not coloured.

7 Add the oysters, champagne, fish stock and a little salt and freshly ground black pepper to taste. Very lightly poach the oysters for 30 seconds then remove them and set aside in a warm place (this may have to be done in batches).

8 Over a high heat, reduce the cooking liquid by two thirds.

9 Add about two thirds of the cream. Bring to the boil and reduce until the sauce coats the back of a metal spoon.

10 Whip the remaining cream until it forms peaks and fold in the egg yolk.

11 Pour the cream/egg mixture into the sauce. Stir gently and remove from the heat. Taste and correct seasonings.

12 In another pan, gently warm the julienne of leeks in the remaining 30g/1oz (2 Tbl) butter.

Serves 4

Equipment
oven grill/broiler
baking tray/sheet

To serve:

1 Arrange a bed of warm leeks in each oyster shell. Place an oyster on top and coat with sauce.

2 Place the oysters on a baking tray and glaze under the grill until slightly browned (about 2 minutes).

3 Garnish with fresh chervil sprigs and, if using, a little sevruga caviar — serve immediately.

NOTES

Among the many varieties of fresh oysters available, there are two main categories. Rock oysters, as the name implies, are grown along rocky coastlines. They have rougher, deeper shells and a slightly more salty taste than the native oysters, reared from indigenous stock farther out to sea. Native oysters have smoother, more saucer-shaped shells and a slightly more delicate flavour. One may be substituted for the other depending on availability.

Caviar generally refers to salted and processed sturgeon eggs. Most are pasteurized to prolong shelf-life but the more delicate, fresh variety is considered superior. Several types are available. Beluga, the most fragile and expensive variety, comes from the largest type of sturgeon (weighing up to 800kg/1750lbs). The eggs are large, well separated and dark grey. Oscietre, considered the most flavourful, has slightly smaller eggs of a grey-brown to golden colour. Sevruga is the most widely available and has the smallest eggs, dark grey and well flavoured. Pressed caviar is produced by pressing together small and less than perfect eggs. It has a rather jam-like texture and a pronounced salty flavour. It is the type most commonly served in Russia. Recently there have been serious efforts to develop caviar industries in China and the Pacific Northwest. Chinese "Mandarin Caviar", produced from the white sturgeon, is now on the market. Some interesting American types are also available. (Prior to the 1920s, the United States, where caviar was served as a free bar snack, was the principal producer. After the First World War, caviar was catapulted to fame in Paris by the fortuitous combination of Charles Ritz, the Petrossian Brothers and an array of exiled Russian aristocrats.)

CRAB BAKED IN SHELLS OR RAMEKINS

CONTRIBUTED BY MARIE HELVIN, LONDON

1 Preheat oven to 200°C/400°F/Gas Mark 6.

2 In a large bowl combine all the ingredients for the filling.

3 Fold the crab meat into the filling, carefully to avoid shredding it.

4 Divide the mixture among the 6 lightly buttered shells or ramekins.

5 Cover each lightly with the fresh white breadcrumbs and dot with the butter.

6 Bake for 15 minutes until hot and the crumb topping is golden brown.

7 Arrange on individual plates, settling each shell into a folded napkin or small nest of mixed lettuces. Place a lemon wedge on the side and serve immediately.

INGREDIENTS

680g/1lb 8oz fresh hardshell crab meat (white only or a combination of white and brown)

For the filling
170g/6oz (1 cup) chopped celery
2 hard boiled eggs – chopped
1 Tbl minced spring onion/scallion
1 tsp minced fresh parsley
150ml/5fl oz (½ cup + 2 Tbl) mayonnaise
225g/8oz (1 cup) dry breadcrumbs
2 Tbl melted butter
1½ tsp Dijon mustard
1½ tsp Worcestershire sauce
1½ tsp fresh lemon juice
½ tsp salt
a pinch cayenne pepper – or more to taste
a pinch dry thyme (or double amount fresh)

For the topping
60g/2oz (1 cup) fresh white breadcrumbs
30g/1oz (2 Tbl) butter

To serve
mixed lettuces or folded napkins to hold the shells steady
fresh lemon wedges

Serves 6

Equipment
6 × 225g/8oz (1 cup) crab or scallop shells or individual ramekins – lightly buttered

NOTES

The dish may be prepared up to 24 hours in advance, refrigerated and returned to room temperature before final baking, but should not be frozen.

Hardshell crabs are found worldwide in numerous varieties. The most basic distinction is between large-bodied (for example, Atlantic, Dungeness and Blue/Coastal) and long-legged (such as Spider, King and Snow varieties). They all have sweet and succulent meat which is usually removed after initial boiling or steaming and gently picked over to remove any stray pieces of membrane (discarding the sponge-like gills/"deadman's fingers" and hard stone-like head sac). Some species (including the Atlantic and Dungeness) have highly prized soft brown meat in addition to white meat. The coral-coloured roe of the females is considered a delicacy.

Softshell crabs are blue/coastal crabs caught when shedding their shells. They are best sautéed or deep-fried and eaten, soft leather-like shell and all.

Warm Lobster Taco with Yellow Tomato Salsa and Jicama Salad

....

CONTRIBUTED BY CHEF DEAN FEARING
THE MANSION ON TURTLE CREEK, DALLAS, TEXAS, USA

INGREDIENTS

For the salsa
450g/1 lb yellow tomatoes (or
    cherry tomatoes)
1 large shallot – finely chopped
1 large clove garlic – finely
    chopped
2 Tbl finely chopped fresh
    coriander/cilantro
1 Tbl champagne or white wine
    vinegar
2 serrano chillies – seeded and
    finely chopped
2 tsp fresh lime juice
salt to taste
1 Tbl of maple syrup (only if
    tomatoes are not sweet
    enough)

For the tortillas (makes 10–12)
225g/8oz (2 cups) plain/all
    purpose flour – sifted
1 tsp baking powder
½ tsp salt
½ tsp sugar
1 Tbl vegetable shortening
120ml/4fl oz (½ cup) warm water

Continued opposite

Prepare the salsa (at least 2 but not more than 8 hours before serving):

1 Place the tomatoes in the food processor and process until well chopped but do not purée. For a crunchier, more typical salsa, put the tomatoes through the fine die of a food grinder.
2 In a bowl, combine the tomatoes and their juice with the other ingredients, adding maple syrup, if needed, to balance and sweeten the flavours. Cover and refrigerate.
3 Adjust seasonings just before serving.

Prepare the tortillas:

1 Sift the flour, baking powder, salt and sugar into a large bowl.
2 Cut in the shortening until the flour looks as though it has small peas in it.
3 Add enough warm water to make a soft dough and mix well. Knead on a well-floured board for 3–5 minutes or until shiny and elastic.
4 Cover the dough and let rest for 30 minutes, out of any draught.
5 Form the dough into balls about 5–6cm/2–2⅓in in diameter. On a lightly floured board, roll into thin circles about 18cm/7in across and 0.5cm/¼in thick.
6 Cook on a hot, ungreased skillet/griddle for about 2 minutes or until lightly browned on the edges.
7 Turn and cook on the other side for about 1 minute or until the edges are brown.
8 Stack and wrap tightly in foil. Keep warm, if using immediately, or reserve to be reheated when needed.

Serves 6

Equipment
food processor with steel blade,
or food grinder
skillet/griddle
extra-large pot

NOTES

Adapted from *The Mansion on Turtle Creek Cookbook*, Grove Weidefeld, 1987.

Serrano chillies, available both red and green, are hotter than the more common jalapeño variety.

Jicama is a beige/brown-skinned tuber that tastes something like a cross between an apple and a potato. It is valued for its slightly sweet flavour and crunchy texture. Available in ethnic markets and some supermarkets. Once cut, it must be either quickly dressed or kept in water to prevent discoloration.

Prepare the jicama salad:

1 In a large bowl, combine all the ingredients.

2 Toss to mix well.

Prepare the lobsters and make the dish:

1 Preheat the oven to 150°C/300°F/Gas Mark 2.

2 Bring an extra large pot of lightly salted water to the boil over a high heat.

3 Add the lobsters – cook for about 8 minutes until just done. Drain and let cool slightly.

4 Remove the meat from the tails, being careful not to tear the meat apart, and cut into thin medallions (or medium dice, if the meat breaks up).

5 Meanwhile, warm the tortillas by placing them (in the foil packet) in the oven for 10–15 minutes.

6 In a medium sauté pan over medium heat, heat the oil. Add the lobster meat and sauté until just heated through.

7 Spoon equal portions of warm lobster into the centre of each warm tortilla – sprinkle with equal portions of grated cheese and shredded spinach.

8 Roll the tortillas up and place in the centre of warm serving plates with the closed edges on the bottom.

9 Surround each taco with salsa, garnish with a small mound of jicama salad and serve immediately.

Lobsters may be boiled a day ahead – remove and slice tail meat, cover and refrigerate. Jicama salad may be prepared several hours ahead and refrigerated, in which case omit salt until almost ready to serve. Cheese and spinach may be shredded several hours ahead – wrap tightly and refrigerate.

Jalapeño Jack cheese is Monterey Jack cheese containing slivers of jalapeño chillies. It has quite a strong spicy flavour. If unavailable, substitute grated Monterey Jack or Cheddar cheese tossed with slivers of fresh hot chillies to taste.

INGREDIENTS

For the jicama salad

½ small jicama – peeled and cut into fine strips

½ small red bell pepper – seeds and membranes removed and flesh cut into fine strips

½ small yellow bell pepper – seeds and membranes removed and flesh cut into fine strips

½ small courgette/zucchini (only the part that has green skin attached) – cut into fine strips

½ small carrot – peeled and cut into fine strips

4 Tbl cold-pressed groundnut/peanut oil

2 Tbl fresh lime juice

salt and cayenne pepper to taste

For the lobster

4 × 450g/1 lb live lobsters

3 Tbl corn oil

120g/4oz (1 cup) grated Jalapeño Jack cheese

60g/2oz (1 cup) shredded fresh spinach leaves – carefully washed and dried before shredding

CHINESE SHRIMP SALAD

CONTRIBUTED BY ALISON PRICE, LONDON

INGREDIENTS

900g/2 lb large prawns/shrimp –
cooked
225g/8oz (1½ cups) mangetout/
snow peas
225g/8oz (2 cups) carrots – cut
into 5cm/2in sticks
2 red bell peppers – cut into
5cm/2in sticks
115g/4oz (2 cups) bean sprouts –
washed and dried
salt and freshly ground pepper to
taste

For the dressing
2 Tbl Japanese rice wine vinegar
1 tsp chilli oil (for home-made see
below)
2 Tbl dark soy sauce
2 cloves garlic – finely chopped
1 tsp Dijon mustard
2 Tbl fresh lime juice
300ml/10fl oz (1¼ cups) good
non-scented oil

To garnish
1 Tbl white sesame seeds – lightly
toasted

Prepare the dressing:
1 Place the vinegar, chilli oil, soy sauce, garlic, mustard and lime juice in a food processor or blender.
2 Process until thoroughly blended then slowly add the oil.
3 Pour the dressing into a storage container – do not refrigerate.

Marinate the prawns/shrimp:
1 Peel the cooked prawns/shrimp leaving the tail-fan shell on. Coat with half of the dressing, cover and refrigerate for 5 hours.

Make the salad:
1 Blanch the mangetout in boiling water for 30 seconds. Refresh in iced water, dry well and cut into 1cm/½in pieces.
2 In a serving bowl, combine the mangetout, carrots, peppers and bean sprouts. Season and toss with the remaining dressing.
3 Drain the marinade from the shrimp and arrange the shrimp on top of the vegetables.
4 Scatter toasted sesame seeds over the salad and serve.

To prepare home-made chilli oil:
1 In a saucepan, heat 300ml/10fl oz (1¼ cups) of groundnut/peanut oil over low heat.
2 Add 1 Tbl dried red chilli flakes (the flakes should foam but not burn – test a few first).
3 Remove the pan from the heat, cover and allow to cool.
4 Add 1 Tbl sesame oil and let the chilli oil sit for 24 hours.
5 Strain through a muslin-lined sieve and store in a tightly sealed glass jar in a cool, dark place, preferably not a refrigerator.

Serves 6 to 8

Equipment
food processor or blender

NOTES

Chilli oil is a fiery seasoning used throughout Asia. It is available, in small bottles, at oriental markets and most supermarkets. You can also make it at home, as described here.

To serve bell peppers raw it is best to first dip them (whole) into boiling water for 1–2 seconds to mellow the flavour and remove the oil which some people find difficult to digest.

To toast sesame seeds pour them into a dry, heavy frying pan and place over a medium heat. Stir constantly until they begin to brown and become very fragrant – remember that they will continue to brown for a few seconds after being removed from pan. Cool on kitchen paper.

Ragoût of Pork, Scallops and Monkfish

CONTRIBUTED BY CHEF DAVID WILSON
THE PEAT INN, FIFE, SCOTLAND

INGREDIENTS

225g/8oz belly pork – diced into
   1cm/½in squares
enough chicken stock to cover the
   pork (approximately 300ml/10fl
   oz/1¼ cups)
1 Tbl virgin olive oil
120g/4oz monkfish fillet – in 12
   thin slices
8 large scallops – sliced in half

For the spicy vinaigrette
4 Tbl white wine vinegar
dash of light soy sauce
dash of balsamic vinegar –
   optional
120ml/4fl oz (½ cup) virgin
   olive oil
salt and freshly ground black
   pepper to taste

To garnish
deep-fried fresh herbs such as
   lovage or basil leaves

1 In a saucepan, cover the pork with the stock and gently simmer until very tender (approximately 45–60 minutes).
2 Preheat the oven grill/broiler.

Prepare the spicy vinaigrette:
1 In a heatproof bowl, combine the white wine vinegar, soy sauce, balsamic vinegar (if using) and a small pinch of salt.
2 Gradually whisk in the olive oil (incorporating each addition fully before adding the next). Taste and adjust seasoning.
3 Warm over simmering water or leave in a warm place.

Make the dish:
1 Strain the pork and arrange the pieces on a baking tray. Grill until crisp (5 minutes under a very hot grill). Keep warm.
2 Meanwhile, in a frying pan, heat the oil until almost smoking. Add the slices of monkfish and sauté until just cooked through (approximately 2 minutes on each side). Remove fish and keep warm.
3 Place the scallop pieces in the same pan and sauté in the hot oil (approximately 30 seconds on each side).
4 Arrange the pork in the centre of 4 warmed individual serving plates. Top with fish and scallop pieces, spoon warm vinaigrette over and around and garnish with deep-fried herbs. Serve immediately.

Serves 4

Equipment
oven grill/broiler

NOTES

Monkfish (anglerfish/lotte) has a sweet taste and firm, slightly chewy texture reminiscent of lobster. A uniquely ugly creature, it has an enormous head, very large mouth filled with needle-like teeth and a scaleless brownish body. Usually only the tail meat is used. After skinning, the tail meat is revealed to be covered with a blue-grey membrane. This must be removed before cooking and then the two fillets easily sliced off the one central cartilaginous bone.

BAKED SARDINES

....

CONTRIBUTED BY CHEF ANTON MOSIMANN
MOSIMANN'S, LONDON

1 Preheat the oven to 180°C/350°F/Gas Mark 4.

2 Scale the sardines by rubbing them with your fingers. Be sure to rub them gently enough not to tear their delicate skin.

3 Season the fish and brush with ½ Tbl of the oil.

4 Combine the tomatoes, garlic, onion, parsley, dill and white wine — season to taste.

5 Brush a shallow ovenproof dish with the remaining oil and pour in the sauce mixture. Place the sardines on top, pushing them down into the sauce.

6 Cook for 5 to 6 minutes only.

7 Cool the sardines for a few minutes, then serve them, still warm, with a plate of lemon wedges on the table.

Serves 4

Equipment
shallow ovenproof dish

INGREDIENTS

....

1kg/2 lbs 3oz fresh sardines —
    gutted with heads removed
1 Tbl olive oil
150g/5oz (¾ cup) peeled,
    seeded and diced tomatoes
1 clove garlic — finely chopped
60g/2oz (½ cup) finely chopped
    onion
3 Tbl fresh finely chopped parsley
1½ Tbl fresh finely chopped dill
120ml/4fl oz (½ cup) dry
    white wine
salt and freshly ground black
    pepper to taste

To garnish
lemon wedges

Serve with
crusty bread

NOTES

Sardines, immature pilchard, are thought to have been named after the island of Sardinia around which they were once found in abundance. The fish develops its rich oily flavour as it grows. Small sardines (Italian sardines) are not very oily and dry out easily, hence they are often served with an oil-based dressing; medium sardines (around 20cm/8in) are more flavourful and preferred for frying or grilling; the largest (Brittany sardines) are very flavourful and can be grilled in their own oil. Baby Atlantic or Pacific herrings and sprats are also sometimes labelled as sardines and have a similar taste.

SMOKED HADDOCK IN SHELLS

CONTRIBUTED BY THE COUNTESS OF AIRLIE, LONDON

INGREDIENTS

2 smoked haddock on the bone
2 tomatoes – peeled, seeded and
    cut into small pieces
10 button mushrooms – cut into
    small pieces
several pinches of fennel seeds
300ml/10fl oz (1¼ cups)
    double/heavy cream
freshly ground black pepper to
    taste

To garnish
a sprinkling of chopped fresh
    fennel or parsley leaves
watercress to steady the shells

Serve with
small fresh rolls and creamed
    spinach

1 Preheat the oven to 200°C/400°F/Gas Mark 6.
2 Carefully remove the haddock flesh from the bones. Break the flesh into small pieces.
3 Arrange the scallop shells on a baking tray and divide the haddock among them.
4 Distribute the tomato and mushrooms over the haddock, then sprinkle with the fennel seeds. Pour over just enough cream to cover all the ingredients. (Whole or semi-skimmed milk can be used instead if preferred.)
5 Bake in the oven for 10 to 15 minutes.
6 Season with pepper to taste and serve immediately, arranged on individual nests of watercress to hold them steady.

Serves 8

Equipment
8 scallop shells
baking tray/sheet

NOTES

Serves 4 as a main course.

Haddock is a smallish member of the cod family with a distinctive "thumb print" marking on its sides. In its fresh state the delicate white flesh can be prepared using any cod recipe. The fish is especially popular smoked: soon after being caught it is cleaned, cut lengthways, salted or dipped in brine and hung by the tail in a smokehouse for 24 hours. Smoked haddock is highly praised for its distinctive flavour and texture; the most celebrated are from the village of Finnan, near Aberdeen, and are marketed as "Finnan Haddies".

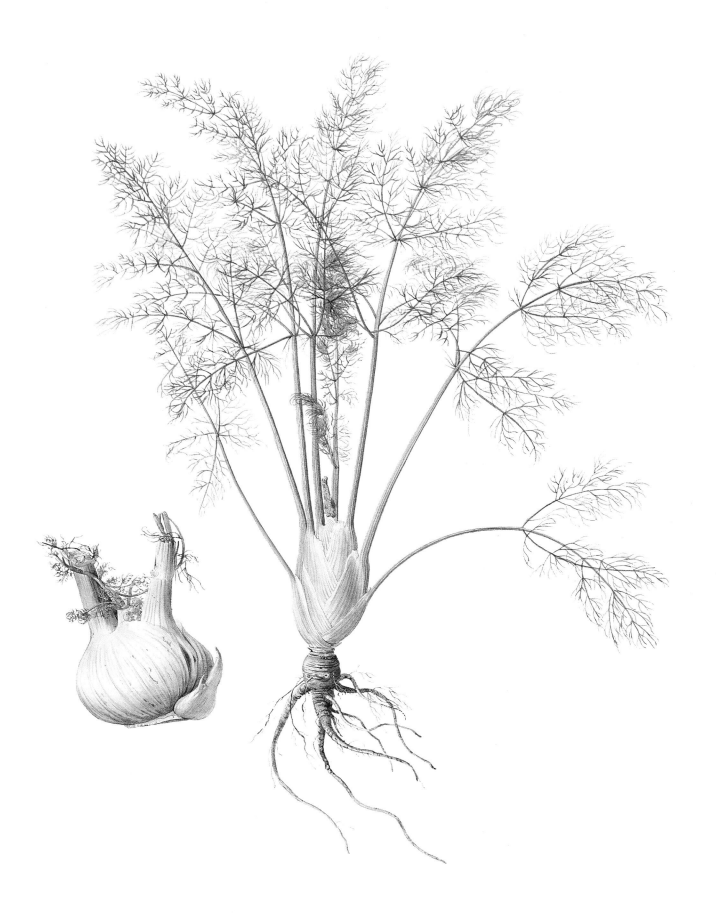

SOUFFLÉS WITH SWISS CHEESE

CONTRIBUTED BY CHEF ALBERT ROUX
LE GAVROCHE, LONDON

INGREDIENTS

150g/5oz (10 Tbl) butter
65g/2¼oz (2/3 cup) plain/all
    purpose flour – sifted
700ml/1¼ pints (3 cups) milk
5 egg yolks
6 egg whites
1 litre/34fl oz (4¼ cups)
    double/heavy cream
200g/7oz (1¾ cups) finely grated
    Gruyère or Emmental cheese
salt and freshly ground white
    pepper to taste

Serve with
warm French bread or, if you want
    to serve this as a main course,
    add a fresh spinach and
    mushroom salad

1 Arrange a shelf in the lower half of the oven and preheat to 200°C/400°F/Gas Mark 6.

2 In a small saucepan, melt 60g/2oz (4 Tbl) of the butter. Add the flour and stir continuously over a gentle heat for 2–3 minutes to make a roux. Remove the pan from the heat and leave to cool slightly.

3 In a separate saucepan, bring the milk to the boil. Whisking constantly, pour it slowly into the roux. Stirring continuously, over high heat, bring to the boil and cook for 3 minutes.

4 Remove the pan from the heat and stir in the egg yolks with salt and white pepper to taste. Dot the surface of the mixture with 15g/½oz (1 Tbl) of the butter in small pieces (this will prevent a skin from forming) – set aside at room temperature.

5 Remove the tins from the refrigerator, grease generously with the remaining butter and place on a baking tray.

6 In a clean dry bowl, beat the egg whites with a pinch of salt until they form stiff peaks.

7 Pour the soufflé mixture into a large bowl. Using a whisk, quickly beat in about a third of the stiffened egg white. With a spatula, carefully fold in the remainder.

8 Using a large spoon, heap the mixture into large mounds in the tartlet tins. Bake the soufflés for 3 minutes, or until the tops begin to turn golden – watch them carefully.

9 Meanwhile, pour the cream into a shallow ovenproof dish large enough to hold the tartlet tins, lightly salt and warm gently without letting the cream boil.

10 Remove the tartlets from the oven. Protecting your hands with a cloth, turn out each soufflé into the dish of warm cream. Sprinkle the cheese over them and place in the oven for 5 minutes.

11 The soufflés must be taken immediately to the table. Using a spoon and fork, gently place them on heated serving plates, taking care not to crush them.

Serves 8

Equipment
8 × 8cm/3in non-stick tartlet tins,
    chilled in the refrigerator
shallow ovenproof dish (large
    enough to hold the tartlet tins)

NOTES

Soufflé Suissesse (French)

Serves 4 as a main course.

Adapted from New Classic Cuisine, QED Publishing Corporation, 1983.

This is an original way of serving cheese soufflés: the cheese is not incorporated but used to glaze them. As they cook the soufflés absorb the cream and become very rich. Always cook soufflés in the lower half of your oven, where the heat is more even.

SPINACH DIP

....

CONTRIBUTED BY DOMINICK DUNNE, CONNECTICUT, USA

1 Thaw the spinach.

2 Using your hands, squeeze the spinach dry and place it in a food processor or blender.

3 Add the remaining ingredients and process until thoroughly combined.

4 Cover and refrigerate for at least 1 hour.

5 Scoop out the red bell pepper or hollow out the red cabbage and, using it as a vegetable "bowl", fill with the green dip.

6 Place the vegetable "bowl" on a large serving plate, surround by mounds of colourful crudités, crackers, tortillas and crisps for dipping, and serve.

Makes 900g/32oz (4 cups) of dip

Equipment
food processor or blender

INGREDIENTS

....

285g/10oz frozen chopped spinach
470ml/16fl oz (2 cups) sour cream
225g/8oz (1 cup) mayonnaise
6 Tbl chopped fresh parsley
90g/3oz (½ cup) chopped spring onions/scallions
4 Tbl packaged dry leek soup mix
1 tsp dry dill weed
1 tsp dry Italian salad dressing mix

To serve
large red bell pepper or small red cabbage
water biscuits/crackers, tortillas, crisps/potato chips and/or crudités for dipping

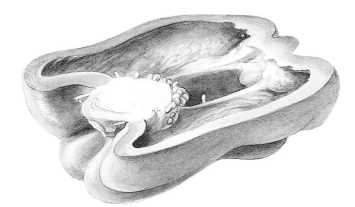

FISH

DEEP-FRIED SNAPPER WITH THREE SAUCES

CONTRIBUTED BY THE HOTEL MERIDIEN BAAN BORAN
THE GOLDEN TRIANGLE, THAILAND

INGREDIENTS

For the tangy red sauce
4 Tbl sesame oil
10g/¼ oz (1/4 cup) dried Chinese
   mushrooms – finely chopped
1 tsp fresh ginger in fine strips
½ tsp finely chopped garlic
265ml/9fl oz (1 cup + 2 Tbl)
   unsalted chicken stock
2 tsp caster/superfine sugar
4 Tbl light soy sauce
4 Tbl oyster sauce
2 tsp cornflour/cornstarch blended
   with 2 Tbl water

For the chilli sauce
4 Tbl vegetable oil
½ tsp finely chopped garlic
½ tsp finely chopped pickled garlic
1 Tbl finely chopped fresh red
   chillies
4 Tbl tamarind juice
2 Tbl fish sauce (nam pla or nuoc
   mam)
4 Tbl white vinegar
½ tsp caster/superfine sugar
a large pinch of freshly ground
   white pepper

Continued opposite

Prepare the tangy red sauce:
1 In a wok, heat the sesame oil. Add the mushrooms, ginger and garlic and stir-fry briefly until fragrant but not coloured.
2 Add the stock, reduce heat and cook, uncovered, for 5 minutes.
3 Add the sugar, soy and oyster sauces and the blended cornflour and water. Stir until the sauce boils and thickens.
4 Pour into a heatproof bowl and reserve (keep warm by placing the bowl in a pan of hot water).

Prepare the chilli sauce:
1 In a wok, heat the vegetable oil. Add the garlic, pickled garlic and chilli and stir-fry until fragrant but not coloured.
2 Add the tamarind juice, fish sauce, vinegar, sugar and white pepper and bring to the boil.
3 Pour into a heatproof bowl and reserve (keep warm by placing in the pan of hot water with the tangy red sauce).

Serves 4

Equipment
large wok or pan to deep-fry the
   whole fish
3 heatproof bowls and a pan that
   will hold them in hot water

NOTES

Pla Saam Rod (Thai)

Chinese mushrooms are sold dry in most oriental markets. They should be soaked in warm water for 30 minutes, drained and tough stems removed before using.

Pickled garlic is sold in jars in most oriental markets.

Tamarind is the pod-like brown fruit of an evergreen tree grown throughout the tropics. The pulp is sold packaged in compressed blocks. To extract the sour concentrate, cut off 50g/2oz of the block, cover with hot water and leave for 20 minutes to dissolve, mashing occasionally with a fork. Strain the resulting liquid and discard the pulp and seeds.

Fish sauce (nam pla/nuoc mam) is a staple of Southeast Asian cuisine and can be found in all oriental markets. It is a thin, brown sauce made from fermented fish, prawns or squid. Characterized by a salty flavour and pungent aroma, it comes in various strengths, and is made into a dipping sauce by adding water, citrus juice and fresh chopped chillies and/or herbs.

Prepare the sweet and sour sauce:

1 In a wok, heat the vegetable oil. Add the tomato, pineapple, cucumber, onion and pepper and stir-fry until fragrant but not coloured.

2 Add the ketchup, sugar, vinegar and soy, chilli and plum sauces and stir until the sauce boils and thickens.

3 Pour into a heatproof bowl and reserve (keep warm by placing the bowl in the pan of hot water with the other sauces).

Cook the fish:

1 Rinse the fish under cold water and pat dry.

2 In a large wok, heat the cooking oil.

3 Dust the fish with flour.

4 Carefully place the whole fish in the hot oil – fry gently on both sides until golden brown and tender (approximately 15 minutes). Meanwhile check that the sauces are hot.

5 Remove the fish from the wok and drain on kitchen paper.

6 Arrange the fish on a serving platter and pour the three sauces over it in stripes.

7 Garnish the tangy red sauce stripe with some coriander leaves and the chilli sauce stripe with finely shredded kaffir lime leaves. Drizzle the coconut milk over the whole fish in a thin trickle and serve immediately.

Snappers, available in numerous varieties, colours and sizes worldwide, have lean firm flesh with a mild excellent flavour. These popular fish are characteristically plump with large heavy heads and dog-like teeth which give them their common name. Some varieties of grouper closely resemble snapper and could be substituted, as could any other moist delicate fish.

Kaffir lime leaves are widely available in oriental markets. They may be frozen for longer-term storage.

INGREDIENTS

For the sweet and sour sauce
4 Tbl vegetable oil
1 tsp finely diced, peeled tomato
1 tsp finely diced fresh pineapple
1 tsp finely diced, peeled and
  seeded cucumber
1 tsp finely diced onion
2 tsp finely diced bell pepper
4 Tbl tomato ketchup
2 tsp caster/superfine sugar
2 Tbl white vinegar
2 Tbl light soy sauce
4 Tbl oriental chilli sauce
3 Tbl sweet plum sauce

For the fish
1kg/2lb 3oz fresh whole snapper –
  cleaned and scaled
2 litres/3½ pints (8½ cups) cooking
  oil
2 Tbl plain/all purpose flour

To garnish
fresh coriander/cilantro leaves –
  chopped
several fresh kaffir lime leaves –
  finely shredded
4 Tbl coconut milk

Serve with
steamed white rice

FILLETS OF SOLE MOTCOMBS

....

CONTRIBUTED BY CHEF GERRY REIDY
MOTCOMBS, LONDON

1 Preheat the oven to 220°C/425°F/Gas Mark 7.

2 Place the fillets in a buttered baking dish with the prawns and scampi arranged on top. Season with black pepper and pour the wine over them.

3 Cover tightly with foil and bake for 8–10 minutes.

4 Remove the foil and carefully drain the cooking liquid into a small saucepan. Place this sauce over high heat to reduce, meanwhile keeping the fish covered and warm.

5 When the cooking liquid has reduced to one third of its volume, whisk in the butter cubes. Remove the pan from the heat to avoid the sauce boiling furiously.

6 Arrange the fish on heated plates, cover with just enough sauce to coat the whole dish, garnish and serve immediately.

INGREDIENTS

2 x 90g/3oz Dover sole fillets –
    skinned
60g/2oz peeled uncooked prawns
2 jumbo peeled uncooked scampi
2 Tbl dry white wine
90g/3oz (6 Tbl) butter – cubed
a pinch of freshly ground black
    pepper

To garnish
a dusting of finely chopped chervil
    or parsley
a few edible flowers

Serve with
runner beans, or an assortment of
    seasonal vegetables

Serves 2

Equipment
an ovenproof dish – buttered

NOTES

Dover Sole, the most celebrated flatfish, boasts both superb flavour and firm delicate texture. True Dover sole comes only from northern European waters (the name reflects a time when Dover was a thriving fishing harbour, rather than the fish's presence in English Channel waters). Unlike other fish, the flavour of Dover sole is said to develop when properly stored for a day or two after being caught. The fish has quite a tough skin, normally removed by the fishmonger. If unavailable, other firm-textured flatfish may be substituted.

The terms "shrimp", "prawn" and "scampi" are used worldwide almost interchangeably to describe numerous small crustaceans. These creatures can come from either fresh or salt water, in an almost infinite variety of sizes and colours, with and without claws and/or sword-like head projections. The correct labelling as to shrimp, prawn or scampi is hopelessly confusing and mostly academic. In common cooking practice, "shrimp" are the smallest, "prawns" are larger and "scampi" are the largest – all are excellent.

Packets of colourful edible flowers are available from greengrocers for use in salads and as garnish. Unless you have been able to research edible flowers thoroughly, these are the only ones to be recommended.

GÂTEAUX OF TURBOT, SALMON AND MUSHROOM BAKED IN FILO PASTRY

CONTRIBUTED BY CHEF MICHAEL FERGUSON
THE YEW TREE INN, ALRESFORD, HAMPSHIRE, ENGLAND

INGREDIENTS

8 large fresh spinach leaves –
  thoroughly washed with tough
  stalks removed
90g/3oz (6 Tbl) unsalted butter
60g/2oz (⅓ cup) finely chopped
  shallots
a little vegetable oil
225g/8oz (2 cups) button
  mushrooms – cleaned, trimmed
  and cut into 6mm/¼in dice
2 tsp finely chopped parsley
60ml/2fl oz (¼ cup) dry white
  wine
90ml/3fl oz (¼ cup + 2 Tbl)
  double/heavy cream
salt and freshly ground white
  pepper to taste

The fish
225g/8oz turbot fillet
225g/8oz skinned salmon fillet

Continued opposite

1 In a large pot of boiling salted water, blanch the spinach leaves for approximately 10 seconds. Quickly remove and plunge them into a bowl of iced water (taking care not to damage them). Carefully lay them on a cloth-covered tray so that they do not touch each other, then place another cloth over the leaves and refrigerate.
2 In a small pan, heat 60g/2oz (4 Tbl) of the butter. Lightly sauté the shallots until softened – set aside.
3 Place a frying pan on the heat – when smoking hot, line it with a little vegetable oil, flash-fry the mushrooms briefly, season and place in a colander to drain.
4 In a saucepan, heat the remaining butter. Allow it to sizzle and start to turn golden brown. Add the mushrooms and sauté briefly. Add the shallots and cook for 2–3 minutes.
5 Add the parsley and white wine and reduce to a syrup.
6 Add the double cream, season and bring to the boil. Reduce the heat and simmer gently until the mixture has the consistency of single cream – pour on a plate to cool.
7 Using tweezers, extract any stray bones from the fish fillets. Slice each fillet into 8 evenly sized medallions 6mm/¼in thick (each gâteau requires 2 turbot and 2 salmon medallions).
8 On a flat work surface, lay 2 slightly overlapping spinach leaves in the centre of a large sheet of greased paper.
9 Place one turbot medallion in the centre of the spinach and season with salt and pepper. Spread a layer of mushroom mixture (about 6mm/¼in thick) over the turbot, season, and place a medallion of salmon on top.
10 Repeat the operation until you have a gâteau of two turbot and two salmon medallions sandwiched together with 3 layers of mushroom mixture (it is important to season every layer).
11 Using the greased/waxed paper for assistance, wrap the spinach around the gâteau to envelop it completely.
12 Prepare 3 more gâteaux, then cover and refrigerate them.

Serves 4

Equipment
baking tray/sheet
greased paper/waxed paper
parchment paper
fine sieve/chinois

NOTES

Turbot, a lozenge-shaped flat fish with succulent firm white flesh, is regarded by many as the finest of all fish. Its leathery brown skin has no scales but instead small bony tubercles. Turbot come in many sizes – the larger are usually cut into manageably sized pieces while the smaller "chicken turbots" are sold whole. The unusual shape and superb reputation of these fish account for the extravagant turbotière (diamond-shaped pans specially for turbot) which take pride of place in many kitchens.

Make the filo parcels:

1 One at a time, enclose the gâteaux in filo pastry: fold a sheet of filo pastry in half, place a gâteau in the centre, wrap the pastry around the gâteau and trim excess away from the seals.

2 Lightly brush the seals with clarified butter to create a firm closure. Brush the surface with clarified butter and place on a baking sheet lined with parchment paper, allowing for equal and generous spacing.

3 Refrigerate for 1 hour.

4 Preheat the oven to 200°C/400°F/Gas Mark 6.

5 Bake the parcels for approximately 15 minutes (test with a cocktail stick/toothpick: when hot in the middle they are done). Do not overcook or the fish will become dry.

Meanwhile, prepare the sauce, and finish the dish:

1 In a saucepan, melt 30g/1oz (2 Tbl) of the butter. Add the shallots and leek and gently sauté until soft but not coloured.

2 Add the wine and vinegar and reduce until all the liquid has evaporated. Add the cream and fish stock and cook until slightly reduced.

3 Whisk in the remaining butter pieces in rapid succession. Bring to the boil, remove from the heat and season with lemon juice and salt.

4 Strain through a fine sieve into a jug and keep warm.

5 Cut each gâteau in half and arrange in the centre of 4 heated dinner plates, turning each half slightly outwards to expose the layering.

6 Finish the warm sauce by stirring in two-thirds of the chopped chives – pour the sauce around each gâteau.

7 Heap 5 spoons of diced tomatoes at intervals around each gâteau, garnish each with a plume of dill, sprinkle the remaining chives between the tomatoes and serve at once.

Keep any filo pastry you are not using under a damp towel: it becomes dry and brittle almost immediately when exposed to air.

INGREDIENTS

4 sheets of filo pastry, thawed if necessary
4 Tbl clarified butter

For the sauce
175g/6oz (12 Tbl) unsalted butter – in small pieces
60g/2oz (⅓ cup) finely chopped shallots
30g/1oz (¼ cup) finely chopped white of leek
150ml/5fl oz (½ cup + 2 Tbl) dry white wine
2 Tbl white wine vinegar
2 Tbl double/heavy cream
2 Tbl fish stock
fresh lemon juice to taste
salt and freshly ground white pepper to taste
2 bunches of chives – finely chopped

To garnish
3 ripe tomatoes – peeled, seeded and cut into 6mm/¼in dice
20 small plumes of dill

Serve with
parslied and sautéed leaf spinach

SAUTÉED SALMON WITH CARAMELIZED ONIONS

CONTRIBUTED BY CHEF PIERRE POLLIN
LE TITI DE PARIS, ARLINGTON HEIGHTS, ILLINOIS, USA

INGREDIENTS

2 Tbl olive oil
900g/2lb fresh salmon fillet
    (preferably Norwegian) – sliced
    into 6 individual portions
450g/1lb fresh pasta (such as angel
    hair)

For the onion preserves
30g/1oz (2 Tbl) unsalted butter
340g/12oz (2 cups) onions – finely
    minced
4 Tbl granulated sugar
4 Tbl sherry vinegar

For the sauce
75g/2½oz (5 Tbl) unsalted butter
2 Tbl chopped shallots
2 Tbl sherry vinegar
3 Tbl light soy sauce
120ml/4fl oz (1/2 cup) chicken
    stock
1 tsp tomato ketchup
2 Tbl double/heavy cream
freshly ground black pepper to
    taste

Serve with
fresh asparagus

Prepare a large pot of lightly salted boiling water for last-minute cooking of the pasta.

Prepare the onion preserves:
1 In a frying pan, heat the butter and sauté the onions until softened but not browned (5–10 minutes) – set aside.
2 In a small heavy-bottomed pan, cook the sugar with 1 Tbl of the vinegar until caramelized.
3 Add the remaining 3 Tbl of vinegar and boil for 1 minute.
4 Mixing thoroughly, slowly add the caramelized sugar to the onions.
5 Return the frying pan to the heat and simmer slowly for 3 minutes – set aside, keeping it warm.

Prepare the sauce:
1 In a saucepan, heat 30g/1oz (2 Tbl) of the butter and sauté the shallots until softened but not browned.
2 Add the vinegar and reduce until almost all the liquid has evaporated.
3 Add the soy sauce, stock, ketchup and cream and bring to the boil.
4 Whisking constantly, slowly add the remaining butter. Season with freshly ground pepper to taste – keep warm.

Prepare the fish and pasta:
1 In a frying pan, heat the olive oil and quickly sauté the salmon fillets until slightly crunchy on the outside yet still translucent on the inside.
2 Meanwhile, cook and drain the pasta.
3 Divide the pasta among 6 heated dinner plates. Arrange the salmon fillets on top, place 3 individual tsp of onion preserve equidistant around the outside of each plate, spoon sauce around the fish and drizzle a bit over it, and serve immediately.

Serves 6

NOTES

Salmon, "the King of Fish", comes in two basic groups: the delicate Atlantic (and similar Baltic or Norwegian varieties) and the generally fuller flavoured Pacific (including the sockeye (red), chinook (king), pink, coho (silver) and chum (dog) varieties). Most salmon sold today is farmed; wild salmon, best caught by hook and line, has a full and distinctive flavour and is a delicacy worth seeking out.

Hake with Capers, Saffron and Tomatoes

CONTRIBUTED BY CHEF PIERRE KOFFMANN
LA TANTE CLAIRE, LONDON

INGREDIENTS

4 hake steaks, about 2cm/¾in thick
2 shallots – finely chopped
250ml/8½fl oz (1 generous cup)
   dry white wine
3 Tbl water
a pinch of saffron
50g/1¾oz (3½ Tbl) unsalted butter
   – cut into cubes
50g/1¾oz (3 Tbl) pickled capers
   (preferably "non pareilles")
400g/14oz (1¾ cups) peeled,
   seeded and diced tomatoes
salt and freshly ground black
   pepper to taste

To garnish
1 tsp chopped fresh parsley

Serve with
country-style bread and fresh
   spinach in butter

1 Preheat the oven to 190°C/375°F/Gas Mark 5.
2 Place the fish in a flameproof dish with the shallots, white wine, water, saffron and salt to taste.
3 On the hob, gently bring to simmering point, then cover with foil and bake in the oven for 15 minutes.
4 Transfer the fish to a warm serving dish – keep hot.
5 Over high heat, reduce the cooking juices by half. Whisk in the butter, add the capers and tomatoes, and taste and adjust the seasoning.
6 Pour the sauce over the hake. Sprinkle with chopped parsley and serve at once.

Serves 4

Equipment
flameproof and ovenproof dish

NOTES

Hake is a firm white-fleshed member of the cod family. Abundant in the Bay of Biscay, it is a very popular fish in Portugal and Spain where it is served baked, fried, poached or steamed. It can also be found off the Irish coast.

Saffron, the dried stigmas of the saffron crocus, is the most expensive spice in the world. Each flower must be picked individually and every tiny stigma carefully removed by hand. It takes approximately 10,000 stigmas to produce 50g/2oz of saffron. It has a pungent aroma and slightly bitter flavour that is much prized in many Mediterranean dishes including paella and bouillabaisse.

Capers are the flower buds of a shrub native to the Mediterranean area. Never eaten raw, they are preserved in brine, salt or olive oil to develop their flavour. Capers are available in various sizes, the largest being the most robustly flavoured and the smallest ("non pareilles") the most delicate. Sharp-tasting capers are used to complement rich meats and fish and to liven up sauces and pasta dishes.

LOBSTER AND CLAMS, MEDITERRANEAN STYLE

CONTRIBUTED BY ANNABEL'S, LONDON

Serves 4

Equipment
stockpot or other very large pot
muslin-lined sieve

1 In a very large pot, combine all the court bouillon ingredients – simmer for 10 minutes.

2 Bring the court bouillon to the boil, add the lobsters, cover and cook for 15 minutes (you may need to turn them a few times).

3 Meanwhile, in a large frying pan, heat 30g/1oz (2 Tbl) of the butter, add the shallots and sauté until softened but not browned. Add the white wine, fish stock, thyme and tarragon.

4 In a large pan, sauté the spinach lightly in the remaining 30g/1oz (2 Tbl) of butter – keep warm.

5 Remove the lobsters from the pot, carefully take the flesh from the shells, cover and keep warm.

6 Add the clams to the fish-stock mixture in the frying pan, cover and cook just until the shells open.

7 Remove the clams from the pan – cover and keep warm.

8 Strain the fish stock mixture through a muslin-lined sieve and return to high heat. Reduce to 150ml/5fl oz and stir in the olive oil.

9 Arrange the hot spinach in the middle of 4 heated plates. Place the lobster meat on top of the spinach, surround with clams, cover with the sauce and serve immediately.

INGREDIENTS

2 × 680g/1½ lb uncooked lobsters
400g/14oz small hardshell clams
(preferably Mediterranean)

For the court bouillon
3 litres/5 pints (12½ cups) water
500ml/17fl oz (2 cups + 2 Tbl)
dry white wine
200g/7oz (1¾ cups) chopped
onion
200g/7oz (1¼ cups) chopped
celery
100g/3½oz (½ cup) chopped
carrots
1 star anise
1 sprig of thyme
2 bay leaves
1 tsp whole black peppercorns
1 Tbl sea salt

For the sauce
60g/2oz (4 Tbl) butter
100g/3½ oz (½ cup) chopped
shallots
60ml/2fl oz (¼ cup) dry white
wine
60ml/2fl oz (¼ cup) fish stock
1 sprig of thyme
1 sprig of fresh tarragon
200g/7oz (8 cups) fresh spinach
leaves – washed
4 Tbl olive oil

Continued overleaf

NOTES

Lobsters are renowned delicacies. These marine crustaceans come in hundreds of varieties but three main types:

Clawed lobsters — with two large front claws (differing in size and function: the larger one with heavy molar-like teeth is for crushing; the smaller, with sharp pointed teeth, is for ripping — beware of both!). The most succulent are 450–550g/1–1¼lb females from very cold water (warm-water lobsters have softer shells and less firm flesh).

Spiny/rock lobsters — with rough shells and no large front claws. They are prized for their succulent tail meat.

Flat/slipper lobsters, often called "Bugs" — these also lack large front claws. Although they have less meat than spiny lobsters, the meat has an excellent flavour. "Bugs" are particularly popular in Australia.

Clams are edible bivalve molluscs found in coastal waters worldwide in a huge variety of types and sizes. Some of the basic types are:

Hardshell/littleneck clams — these can seal their shells tightly. They come in many sizes from the tiny Italian vongole to the large quahog/horse/chowder clams of New England.

Softshell/longneck clams — these have brittle thin shells and a protruding siphon which prevents the shell from closing completely. The dark covering of the siphon is peeled off before eating.

Razor clams — these have sharp-edged brittle shells (resembling old-fashioned straight-edged razors) that permanently "gap" open. They are considered a rare delicacy and like all clams must never be overcooked lest they turn tough and rubbery.

Geoduck — these have large protruding siphons (several feet in length when fully grown). The siphon is peeled and the meat sliced and pounded into geoduck (pronounced gouie-duck) "steaks".

Star anise (Chinese anise) is the brown, star-like, eight-pointed seed pod from an Asian evergreen shrub (a member of the evergreen magnolia family). Each branch of the star contains a shiny brown seed. The pod (whole or in parts) and the individual seeds are used to impart a rich licorice-like aromatic flavour. Star anise is available in the spice section of oriental markets and large supermarkets. It is unrelated to Western anise although the taste is similar.

GRILLED TUNA WITH ASPARAGUS SALAD AND CREOJA SAUCE

CONTRIBUTED BY CHEF HUBERT KELLER
FLEUR DE LYS, SAN FRANCISCO, CALIFORNIA, USA

INGREDIENTS

1 small head each of: radicchio,
   lettuce, chicory/Belgian endive
4 fresh tuna steaks (approximately
   150g/5oz each)
24 fresh asparagus tips
1 ripe tomato – peeled, seeded
   and diced

For the creoja sauce
1 Tbl finely chopped red onion
1 Tbl finely chopped celery
1 Tbl finely chopped carrot
1 Tbl finely chopped green bell
   pepper
2 Tbl finely chopped tomato flesh
1 Tbl finely chopped chives
1 Tbl finely chopped
   coriander/cilantro
1 Tbl finely chopped parsley
120ml/4fl oz (½ cup) hazelnut oil
3 Tbl sherry or champagne
   vinegar

For the vinaigrette
juice of 1 lemon
5 Tbl extra virgin olive oil
1 clove garlic – chopped
1 branch fresh thyme
1 branch fresh coriander/cilantro
1 bay leaf

salt and freshly ground black
   pepper to taste

Continued opposite

Prepare the creoja sauce:

1 In a bowl, combine the onion, celery, carrot, green pepper, tomato, chives, coriander and parsley, season with salt and freshly ground black pepper and mix lightly.

2 In a separate bowl, beat the oil and vinegar together, then pour over the vegetables. Stir to mix.

3 Cover and set aside at room temperature for 1 hour before serving.

Prepare the dish:

1 Wash and thoroughly dry the radicchio, lettuce and chicory/Belgian endive. Wrap in a clean towel and place in the refrigerator to crisp for 1 hour.

2 Preheat the oven to 190°C/375°F/Gas Mark 5.

3 Prepare the vinaigrette: in a small bowl, whisk together the lemon juice and olive oil and season with salt and freshly ground black pepper. Add the remaining ingredients and combine well – reserve.

4 Place the tuna steaks on a plate, evenly coat with 2 Tbl of the vinaigrette, cover and leave to marinate for at least 20 minutes.

5 Poach or steam the asparagus until just tender (approximately 7 minutes – try one to make sure because the timing depends on size). Drain, refresh in cold water, drain again, place on a clean towel and gently pat dry. Transfer to a shallow bowl, coat with a little vinaigrette and leave to marinate.

Serves 4

Equipment
grill/broiler, grill pan or barbecue

Prepare the croûtons:

1 Brush the bread pieces lightly on both sides with olive oil and arrange on a baking tray.

2 Toast in the preheated oven until crisp and golden (approximately 5 minutes per side). Reserve.

Prepare the tuna:

1 Preheat the grill/broiler, grill pan or barbecue until very hot and grill or broil the tuna steaks for no longer than 2–3 minutes per side (tuna tends to be dry if overcooked, so serve it medium to medium-rare).

Assemble the dish:

1 Place the salad greens in a large mixing bowl and toss thoroughly with the remaining vinaigrette.

2 Spread the croûtons with tapenade.

3 Place the salad leaves in the centre of each dinner plate, arranging the asparagus tips attractively to one side of the leaves.

4 Top the leaves with a tuna steak, spoon the creoja sauce halfway over each steak, decorate with two croûtons and 1 Tbl of diced tomato, and serve immediately.

INGREDIENTS

For the croûtons
8 thin slices French bread
virgin olive oil
3 Tbl Tapenade

NOTES

Tuna is found worldwide in a number of species and sizes. The rich, dark red flesh is extremely delicate and should be handled gently and eaten as fresh as possible. The most readily available types are bluefin, blackfin (bigeye), skipjack (bonito) and yellowfin (aku). All are delicious grilled. Because tuna takes on a steak-like quality when it is grilled medium-rare, it often can be paired with fairly meaty wines such as Cabernets or Cabernet/Merlot blends.

Tapenade, a Provence speciality, is a spicy combination of capers, anchovies and black olives. It is available, freshly made or in jars, in some gourmet shops.

FILLET OF RED MULLET VINAIGRETTE

....

CONTRIBUTED BY CHEF ALLAN HOLLAND

MALLORY COURT HOTEL, LEAMINGTON SPA, WARWICKSHIRE, ENGLAND

INGREDIENTS

4 x 225g/8oz red mullets – filleted
and small bones tweezed out
(reserve heads and bones for
fish stock)

For the vinaigrette dressing
1 tomato – peeled, seeded and
finely chopped
1 bunch of basil – finely chopped
265ml/9oz (1 cup + 2 Tbl) extra
virgin olive oil
¼ clove garlic – finely chopped
1 small shallot – finely chopped
1 tsp sherry vinegar
2 bay leaves

salt and freshly ground black
pepper to taste

For the fish stock
reserved heads and bones from
the mullets (plus a few more if
your fishmonger has them);
1 small roughly chopped onion;
1 sliced carrot; 1 sliced celery
stalk; 2 parsley stalks; 1 bay leaf;
1 fresh thyme stalk; 8 whole
black peppercorns

To garnish
4 black olives
1 Tbl fresh basil leaves – shredded
4 cherry tomatoes

Prepare the vinaigrette dressing, several days in advance:
1 Combine all the ingredients and add salt and pepper to taste.
2 Leave at room temperature for 4 to 5 days to macerate.

Prepare the fish stock:
1 Put all ingredients into a large pot, cover with cold water
and over high heat bring to a rapid boil, skimming off any foam
that rises to the surface.
2 Lower the heat and simmer for no more than 20 minutes.
(If fish bones are simmered for more than 20 minutes the stock
may turn bitter – after bones are removed, however, stock can
be further reduced without damaging its flavour.)
3 Strain the stock. (Later, after steaming, keep the stock that is
left by allowing it to cool then pouring it into ice-cube trays
and freezing as "stock cubes".)

Steam the fish and serve:
1 Using the fish stock, instead of water, as the steaming
medium, bring the steamer to the boil. Depending on your
steamer, you may need to add water to the fish stock.
2 Season the red mullet fillets with salt and pepper and steam
over fish stock for 3 to 5 minutes. Turn heat off and allow the
fillets to rest in the steamer for 5 minutes.
3 Remove the bay leaves from the dressing. Spoon the dressing
on to warmed serving plates and arrange the fish fillets on top.
Garnish with olives, shredded basil and cherry tomatoes and
serve immediately.

Serves 4

Equipment
steamer

NOTES

Serves 8 as a starter.

Red mullets (goatfish) have been
highly valued, especially in the
Mediterranean region, since
Roman times. These small fish
have firm savoury flesh, and are
nicknamed "the woodcock of the
sea" because they too are often
prepared ungutted. Red mullets
have almost ridged bodies, two
barbels under their chin and bright
red skin (the brilliant colour of
which is a sure sign of freshness).
Not to be confused with the
unrelated grey mullets, which are
similar to bass, have soft flesh and
sometimes a slightly "muddy"
taste.

STEAMED LAPU-LAPU IN BANANA LEAVES

....

CONTRIBUTED BY THE MANILA HOTEL, MANILA, PHILIPPINES

INGREDIENTS

600g/20oz filleted fish (preferably lapu-lapu but red snapper, turbot, halibut or any other firm white fish may be substituted)

⅛ tsp salt

⅛ tsp freshly ground black pepper

¼ tsp Worcestershire sauce

½ tsp fresh lemon juice

30g/1oz (2 Tbl) unsalted butter

1 Tbl finely minced garlic

30g/1oz (3 Tbl) finely chopped onion

30g/1oz (3 Tbl) finely chopped carrot

30g/1oz (3 Tbl) finely chopped leek

30g/1oz (3 Tbl) finely chopped celery

30g/1oz (3 Tbl) finely chopped green mango

additional salt, freshly ground pepper and Worcestershire sauce to taste

1.2m/4 ft fresh banana leaves

Continued opposite

1 Depending upon the type of fish you are using – remove the skin and tweeze out any stray bones.

2 Season the fish with salt, pepper, Worcestershire sauce and lemon juice – cover and refrigerate until needed.

3 In a saucepan heat the butter and briefly sauté the garlic until softened.

4 Add the finely chopped vegetables and mango to the pan, season with salt, pepper and a few drops of Worcestershire sauce to taste and sauté until just softened and fragrant – remove from heat, cool and reserve.

5 In a large pot of boiling water, lightly blanch the banana leaves, refresh under cold running water and pat dry.

6 With a sharp knife or scissors, trim the leaves into 4 x 30cm (1 foot) squares, removing any tough centre ribs.

7 Lightly coat each fish fillet with the vegetable mixture and wrap individually in a piece of banana leaf, securing the loose end with a wooden cocktail stick if necessary. Place in the refrigerator until needed. (The banana parcels can be prepared and refrigerated for several hours before steaming.)

Serves 4

Equipment
steamer
heatproof plate

NOTES

Lapu-lapu, one of the most famous fish in the Philippines, is a large, white- and beige-striped, bigmouth fish that rather resembles a grouper. The flesh is white with a delicate flavour which is so highly praised that it is most often served for special occasions and celebrations. Substitute any high quality white fish in this delicate recipe which is designed to enhance the special clean flavour of fresh fish.

Banana leaves are often used in Asian cooking to wrap steamed dishes and are available in many oriental markets. They are not eaten but do impart a delicate fresh aroma to dishes. If not available, foil or 2 or 3 layers of blanched lettuce leaves can be used as a substitute but the taste and effect will be significantly different.

Prepare the garnish:

1 Preheat the oven to 220°C/425°F/Gas Mark 7.

2 Roast the shrimp paste on a piece of foil for 5 minutes, until fragrant.

3 In a bowl, toss the tomato, pepper and mango slices with the shrimp paste until thoroughly coated – cover and reserve at room temperature.

To serve:

1 Place the wrapped fish fillets on a heatproof plate and steam in a hot steamer until just cooked through. The timing depends on the thickness of the fillets – as a rule of thumb, allow at least 12 minutes per 2.5cm/1in of thickness.

2 Cut the parcels diagonally (remove cocktail sticks), arrange on heated plates, garnish with the vegetable salad and serve immediately.

INGREDIENTS

To garnish
I Tbl shrimp paste
I tomato – thinly sliced
I bell pepper – cored and cut into julienne strips
I green mango – peeled and cut into julienne strips

Serve with
steamed white rice

Green mango, a staple in Asian cooking, is available in many Asian, particularly Thai, markets. It is the green, unripe version of the sweet fruit found in western greengrocers. For this dish ask for a "sour", very hard, mango – the "sweet" variety in Asian markets is often also green, although much more tender to the touch. If unavailable, 2 sour green apples can be substituted.

Shrimp paste is one of the main sources of protein in Southeast Asia. Widely available in Asian markets, it is sold in small airtight containers and comes in various forms, colours and textures. It has an extremely pungent aroma and a strong, very distinctive flavour which is often considered an acquired taste. It keeps well if tightly sealed.

SEABASS WITH HERBS SANTINI

CONTRIBUTED BY SANTINI, LONDON

INGREDIENTS

1 × 1.3kg/2 3/4 lb seabass –
  cleaned and gutted

For the sauce
255ml/9fl oz (1 cup + 2 Tbl)
  extra virgin olive oil
a good squeeze of lemon juice
90ml/3fl oz (6 Tbl)
  Worcestershire sauce
large sprig of rosemary
½ clove garlic – finely chopped
a small bunch of chives – roughly
  chopped
a small bunch of parsley –
  chopped
a few drops balsamic vinegar
a tiny pinch Aromat seasoning –
  dissolved in a little water

To cook the fish
1 onion – quartered
3 whole carrots – scraped
1 bay leaf
1 sprig of parsley
salt and freshly ground black
  pepper

Serve with
boiled potatoes and a green salad

Prepare the sauce, at least 1 day before serving:

1 In a bowl, mix the olive oil, lemon juice and Worcestershire sauce.

2 Strip the leaves from the rosemary and add these, the garlic, chives and parsley to the sauce.

3 Mix in the vinegar and dissolved Aromat and cover – leave in a cool place for at least 24 hours (it is important not to refrigerate it).

Prepare the dish:

1 Place the large shallow pan, or fish kettle, of water on to boil.

2 Add the onion, carrots, bay leaf, parsley and salt and pepper.

3 When the water starts to bubble, turn the heat down very low and place the fish into the pan.

4 Cook gently, with just a slight ripple on the surface of the water, for 10–12 minutes depending on the size of the fish (but not more than 15 minutes).

5 Carefully transfer the fish to a serving dish and very gently lift away the skin from its uppermost side (starting just beneath the gills and ending at the tail – this is rather fiddly, so be patient).

6 Stir the sauce (which will have separated) to incorporate all the ingredients, pour over the seabass and serve at once.

Serves 4 to 5

Equipment
a large shallow pan (preferably a fish kettle) from which the fish can easily be lifted without breaking

NOTES

Branzino Santini (Italian)

"Seabass" refers to saltwater members of the extremely large bass family (which includes freshwater relatives). Seabass are characterized by lean, moist flesh, with a mild delicate flavour that takes beautifully to virtually every method of fish cookery. Rely on your fishmonger to select among the numerous saltwater bass and appropriate substitutes available in your area.

Aromat is a flavour enhancer/ seasoning blend.

Yellowtail on Bamboo Shoot with Seaweed Salad and Ginger Soy Sake Vinaigrette

CONTRIBUTED BY CHEF GUENTER SEEGER
THE DINING ROOM, THE RITZ-CARLTON BUCKHEAD, ATLANTA, GEORGIA, USA

INGREDIENTS

For the seaweed salad
120–175g/4–6oz prepared jellyfish
2 large sheets of nori (dried
   seaweed)
2 tsp rice wine vinegar
1 Tbl sesame oil
cayenne pepper to taste
1 tsp white sesame seeds

For the vinaigrette
100ml/3½fl oz (7 Tbl) sake
4 Tbl light soy sauce
juice of 1 lemon
freshly ground black pepper to
   taste
300ml/10fl oz (1¼ cups)
   grapeseed oil (sunflower or
   avocado oil may be substituted)

Continued opposite

Prepare the seaweed salad:
1 Rinse the dried jellyfish well in cold running water, drain and place in a bowl. Cover with boiling water and soak for 15 minutes or until tender. Drain and continue to soak in at least 6 changes of cold water – just before use, drain thoroughly and pat dry with kitchen paper.
2 Lightly toast the nori sheets by passing their shiny side over an open flame. Using scissors, cut them into julienne strips.
3 In a bowl, whisk together the rice wine vinegar, sesame oil and cayenne pepper to taste.
4 Gently but thoroughly toss the prepared jellyfish and seaweed strips in the dressing.
5 In a dry frying pan, carefully toast the sesame seeds until just golden (stirring constantly, as they burn easily).
6 Just before serving, add the toasted sesame seeds to the salad and toss gently.

Prepare the vinaigrette:
1 In a bowl, whisk together the sake, soy sauce, lemon juice and freshly ground pepper to taste.
2 Gradually whisk in the grapeseed oil until it is thoroughly combined into the vinaigrette.

Serves 6

Equipment
large non-stick sauté pan

NOTES

Jellyfish are sold dry and shreddec in oriental markets.

Nori/laver is dried, processed seaweed in dark green-black sheets resembling handmade paper. Readily available in oriental shops and supermarkets, it should be lightly toasted before use or it will be tasteless and tough. Keep nori tightly sealed and use soon after opening; it is very sensitive to dampness.

Sauté the fish:

1 Season the fish fillets with salt and freshly ground black pepper.

2 Heat a non-stick sauté pan until very hot (note: this recipe uses no oil to sauté the fish).

3 Add the fish fillets and sauté (turning carefully) until just cooked through.

Finish the dish:

1 Rinse the bamboo shoot under cold water (removing any white deposits).

2 Blanch briefly (approximately 1 minute) in a pan of boiling water to which the juice of half a fresh lemon has been added.

3 Immediately drain, and slice lengthways.

4 Divide and arrange the strips of bamboo shoot and the seaweed salad on individual serving plates, set the fish fillets on top, spoon vinaigrette over and serve at once.

INGREDIENTS

6 yellowtail/silver perch fillets
salt and freshly ground black
   pepper
1 bamboo shoot
juice of half fresh lemon

Yellowtail/silver perch is a lean, medium- to firm-textured fish with moist delicate flesh. It is particularly popular in the southeastern United States. If unavailable, substitute another local sweet tender white fish, such as snapper or rockfish.

Bamboo shoots are the tender edible centres of certain varieties of bamboo. "Spring shoots" are quite large and "winter shoots" are slender and more tender. The fresh shoots are laboriously peeled of their tough outer covering and parboiled. Although sometimes available prepared in the chilled section of oriental markets, it is more common to purchase them tinned either whole or sliced.

SHRIMP CREOLE

CONTRIBUTED BY ED BRADLEY, NEW YORK CITY

INGREDIENTS

90g/3oz (6 Tbl) unsalted butter
4 medium onions – finely
    chopped
3 cloves garlic – minced
3 stalks celery – chopped
3 green bell peppers – seeded
    and chopped into 2cm/¾in
    pieces
I fresh jalapeño pepper – seeded
    and minced
4 medium tomatoes – roughly
    cubed
4 Tbl finely chopped fresh parsley
I bay leaf
2 Tbl Matouk's Hot Sauce (or
    more to taste)
900g/2lb uncooked medium
    prawns/shrimp – shelled and
    deveined
salt and freshly ground black
    pepper to taste

To garnish
lemon wedges
fresh parsley

Serve with
white rice

1 In a large saucepan, heat 30g/1oz (2 Tbl) of the butter. Add the onion and garlic and sauté over medium heat for 5 minutes (do not brown).
2 Add the celery and the bell and jalapeño peppers, season with salt and freshly ground black pepper to taste and cook, stirring frequently, for about 4 minutes (do not let the vegetables become soggy; they should remain crisp).
3 Add the tomatoes, parsley and bay leaf, cover and bring to the boil.
4 Lower heat and simmer for 10 minutes.
5 Remove the bay leaf and stir in the Matouk's Hot Sauce.
6 In a large frying pan, heat the remaining 60g/2oz (4 Tbl) butter. Over high heat, sauté the prawns for 1 minute.
7 Pour the tomato mixture over the prawns – stir well and bring just to the boil.
8 Remove from heat and serve immediately on heated plates, garnished with lemon wedges and fresh parsley.

Serves 6

NOTES

Jalapeños, native of Mexico, are the best known and most widely used hot chilli pepper. They are plump, around 8cm/3in long and 2.5cm/1in in diameter, and range from hot to very hot. Unripe jalapeños are dark green; ripe ones, which are slightly sweeter, red. To modify the heat of a chilli pepper, carefully remove and discard the seeds and internal ribs.

Matouk's Hot Sauce is a fiery blend of papaya and hot peppers from Trinidad. It is widely available in gourmet, Indian and West Indian markets. Other similar fruit-based hot pepper sauces could be substituted but not a simple red pepper sauce like Tabasco Sauce.

SCAMPI ALLA CARLINA

CONTRIBUTED BY ARRIGO CIPRIANI
VENICE, ITALY

1 Wash the scampi and dry them well with kitchen paper.

2 Season the scampi with salt and pepper, dredge them in flour and shake in a sieve to remove any excess flour.

3 Heat the oil in a large frying pan over medium-high heat. Add the scampi and cook them in batches, tossing constantly, for 4 or 5 minutes, until they are slightly browned and crisp. Remove with a slotted spoon and arrange in one layer in a shallow serving dish.

4 Pour off the oil from the frying pan, add the butter and parsley, and cook for 30 seconds or so, until the butter just starts to brown. Remove the pan from the heat.

5 Sprinkle the capers and gherkins over the scampi, sprinkle on a few drops of Worcestershire sauce, and dot with tomato sauce.

6 Squeeze on some lemon juice, pour the butter and parsley over all the scampi and serve immediately.

INGREDIENTS

1.1kg/2½lb large, raw scampi/
  Dublin Bay prawns, peeled and
  deveined
flour for dredging
4 to 6 Tbl extra virgin olive oil
60g/2oz (¼ cup) unsalted butter,
  cut into pieces
2 Tbl chopped flat-leaf parsley
1 Tbl chopped drained capers
2 Tbl chopped unsweetened
  gherkins/cornichons
Worcestershire sauce
4 Tbl freshly made tomato sauce
juice of half a lemon
salt and freshly ground black
  pepper to taste

Serves 6

Equipment
large shallow serving dish

NOTES

Adapted from The Harry's Bar Cookbook, Bantam Books, New York, and Smith Gryphon, London.

Scampi alla Carlina was invented by Arrigo Cipriani's sister Carla, "always considered the best cook in the family," he says, and named after her.

GRILLED SCALLOPS IN A LIGHT SOY MOUSSELINE SAUCE

CONTRIBUTED BY CHEF FLORIAN TRENTO
GADDI'S, THE PENINSULA HOTEL, HONG KONG

Serves 4

Equipment
blender
grill/broiler or grill pan

NOTES

To make 2 Tbl fish glaze: In a heavy-bottomed saucepan bring 8 Tbl fish stock to the boil and reduce by three quarters until thick and syrupy, skimming if necessary.

To make tomato peel "flowers": Using a sharp paring knife carefully cut one continuous strip of tomato peel approximately 2cm (less than 1in) wide, starting at the bottom/non-stem end of the tomato and gently rotating the tomato in your hand. Roll the strip around itself, placing the "bottom" end in the centre. The wrap will gently expand when the "flower" is positioned on the dish, and if garnished with green herb leaves takes on the appearance of a rose. Cut the peel with a wavy edge for an even more realistic look.

1 Pat the scallops dry. In a bowl, coat them with olive oil, season with black pepper, cover and marinate for approximately 10 minutes.
2 In a sauté pan, heat 10g/¼oz (½ Tbl) of the butter, add the tomato and sauté briefly. Add the vinegar, fish glaze, soy sauce and Tabasco and bring to the boil.
3 Pour the sauce into a blender, process until very smooth then return to the pan — set aside.

Prepare the garnish:
1 In half the butter, lightly sauté the courgette "spaghetti" until heated through — set aside, keeping warm.
2 In a separate pan, lightly sauté the bean sprouts in the remaining butter until heated through — set aside, keeping warm.

Finish the dish:
1 Preheat the grill/broiler or grill pan.
2 Season the scallops with a little fine sea salt and grill until just cooked through, turning once.
3 Place the sauce on low heat, whisk in the remaining butter and at the last minute, carefully fold in the whipped cream and season to taste.
4 Arrange the strands of courgette in the centre of 4 heated serving plates, garnish with tomato "flowers" and arrange the bean sprouts around the plate.
5 Pour the sauce on top of the bean sprouts.
6 Arrange the grilled scallops on the sauce.
7 Garnish with sprigs of fresh dill and serve at once.

INGREDIENTS

24 fresh scallops – cleaned and trimmed
4 Tbl extra virgin olive oil
120g/4oz (8 Tbl) unsalted butter
4 ripe tomatoes – peeled, seeded and diced
2 Tbl white wine vinegar
2 Tbl fish glaze
6 Tbl light soy sauce
4 dashes Tabasco Sauce
6 Tbl double/heavy cream – whipped
fine sea salt and freshly ground black pepper to taste

To garnish
30g/1oz (2 Tbl) unsalted butter
200g/7oz (4 cups) unpeeled courgette/zucchini – cut lengthways into long very thin strands resembling spaghetti
150g/5oz (2 cups) young bean sprouts – trimmed
4 tomato-peel "flowers"
sprigs of fresh dill

POULTRY

ROAST PARTRIDGE WITH MARINATED GRAPES AND SAUTERNES ESSENCE

CONTRIBUTED BY CHEF STEWART CAMERON
TURNBERRY HOTEL, AYRSHIRE, SCOTLAND

INGREDIENTS

400g/14oz (3½ cups) seedless
    green grapes – peeled
300ml/10fl oz (1¼ cups) Sauternes
    wine
4 young partridges – prepared for
    the oven
4 slices cured pork fat – for
    wrapping the breasts
120g/4oz (8 Tbl) unsalted butter
600ml/1 pint (2½ cups) game
    stock
salt and freshly ground black
    pepper to taste

For the stuffing
30g/1oz (2 Tbl) unsalted butter
60g/2oz streaky bacon – chopped
2 Tbl chopped onion
1 sprig fresh thyme
120g/4oz partridge and chicken
    livers – trimmed and roughly
    chopped
60g/2oz (½ cup) seedless green
    grapes – peeled
salt and freshly ground black
    pepper to taste

To garnish
4 large croûtons
chopped fresh parsley

Marinate the grapes in the Sauternes for 1 hour.

Prepare the stuffing:
1 In a frying pan, heat the butter and sauté the bacon until the fat is just translucent. Add the onion and thyme and continue to sauté until the onion is golden brown.
2 Add the partridge and chicken livers and sauté quickly.
3 Season to taste and then pass through a fine sieve into a bowl. Add the peeled grapes and set aside.

Prepare the dish:
1 Preheat the oven to 190°C/375°F/Gas Mark 5.
2 Thoroughly wash and dry the partridges and season the insides. Carefully fill the breast cavities with stuffing.
3 Season the outside of the birds, wrap the breasts in pork fat and lightly tie up for roasting with kitchen string.
4 In an ovenproof pan, melt 30g/1oz (2 Tbl) of the butter. Add the birds and roll them in the hot butter until sealed.
5 Place in the oven for 20 minutes until the birds are almost cooked, basting occasionally. Then transfer the birds to a clean ovenproof pan, cover and keep in a warm place.
6 Pour off excess fat (but not flavourful juices) from the original pan and return to the heat. Add the Sauternes marinade and 170g/6oz (1½ cups) of the grapes. Scrape the pan gently to incorporate the caramelized roasting bits. Pour in the game stock and cook until reduced by half.
7 Pass through a fine sieve into a clean saucepan – keep warm.
8 Remove the strings and fat slices from the partridges and return them to the oven to finish cooking.
9 Lightly sauté the remaining grapes in 30g/1oz (2 Tbl) of the butter, while whisking the remaining 60g/2oz (4Tbl) butter (cut into pieces) into the warm sauce.
10 Place the croûtons on heated plates and arrange a bird on each. Garnish with the sautéed grapes and a sprinkling of parsley, and serve immediately, with sauce on the side.

Serves 4

Equipment
kitchen string
ovenproof skillet/frying pan
fine sieve/chinois

NOTES

To peel grapes, briefly blanch (no more than 5 seconds) in boiling water then plunge immediately into iced water. Using a small knife, peel from the stem end.

Partridge is a highly prized, delicately flavoured game bird, often considered superior to its close relative the pheasant. Tender-fleshed young birds (which require very little cooking time) can be distinguished by their flexible beaks, pale feet and pointed tail feathers. Older partridges, called "perdix" in French, are best slowly braised for longer periods. In the US, the word "partridge" is mistakenly used to refer to a number of small birds including the ruffed grouse, quail and bobwhite.

ROAST DUCK AND POMEGRANATES IN NUT SAUCE

CONTRIBUTED BY CHEF MICHAEL CARVER

THE WELCOMBE HOTEL AND GOLF COURSE, STRATFORD-UPON-AVON, WARWICKSHIRE, ENGLAND

Serves 4

Equipment
roasting tin/pan with rack

NOTES

Do not be tempted to use an electric juicer for the pomegranates as the bitter pith would then be included – a manual juice squeezer works well.

1 Preheat the oven to 190°C/375°F/Gas Mark 5.

2 Wipe the duckling inside and out, season the cavity with salt and pepper and place the whole onion inside.

3 Truss the duck, prick the skin and rub all over with salt. Place breast-side down on a rack in a roasting tin and add 3 Tbl of water.

4 Roast for 45 minutes, then turn the bird on its back and roast for a further 50 minutes.

5 Meanwhile, place the giblets in a saucepan with the water, bring to the boil and skim off the foam.

6 Cover, lower heat and simmer gently for 45 minutes. Strain the stock – set aside.

Prepare the nut sauce:

1 In a saucepan, melt the butter and fry the onion until golden.

2 Remove the pan from the heat and stir in the walnuts.

3 Return to the heat, add the pomegranate juice, lime juice, sugar and the reserved giblet stock – cover and simmer gently for 30 minutes or until the sauce thickens.

Assemble and serve:

1 When duck is done, remove from the oven. Drain the juices from the duck cavity back into the roasting tin and place the duck on a heated platter – keep warm.

2 Skim off fat from the roasting tin and pour the remaining juices into the sauce. Taste and adjust seasoning and simmer, stirring, for 3 minutes.

3 Joint the duck and arrange on heated plates garnished with pomegranate, lime slices and walnuts. Serve with the sauce.

INGREDIENTS

1 x 2.3kg/5lb duckling – giblets reserved
1 small whole onion – peeled
600ml/1 pint (2½ cups) water for the giblets
salt and freshly ground pepper to taste

For the nut sauce
60g/2oz (4 Tbl) butter
1 onion – finely chopped
175g/6oz (1½ cups) ground walnuts
the juice of 4 pomegranates
2 Tbl fresh lime juice
a large pinch of sugar

To garnish
fresh pomegranate wedges
lime slices
walnuts

BARBARY DUCK

CONTRIBUTED BY CHEF PHILIP BRITTEN
THE CAPITAL HOTEL, LONDON

INGREDIENTS

1 x 1.6kg/3½lb Barbary duck
225g/8oz (1 cup) honey
1 Tbl sea salt
1 Tbl crushed white pepper

Serve with
gratin dauphinois
Brussels sprouts

1 Preheat the oven to 170°C/325°F/Gas Mark 3.

2 Wash the duck and pat dry.

3 Smear the bird with honey and sprinkle with salt and crushed white pepper.

4 Place in a roasting tin and roast for 2 hours, basting every 20 minutes with the pan drippings.

5 Remove from the oven, cover with foil and allow to rest for 10 minutes.

6 Slice into serving portions and serve immediately on well-heated plates with gratin dauphinois and Brussels sprouts.

Serves 3 to 4

Equipment
roasting tin/pan

NOTES

The Barbary duck is a rather large bird, reared in the wild or "free range". It is prized for its firm lean flesh, large breast and slightly gamey flavour.

GUINEA FOWL WITH PEVERADA SAUCE

CONTRIBUTED BY L'INCONTRO, LONDON

1 Preheat the oven to 180°C/350°F/Gas Mark 4.
2 Prepare the stuffing: in a food processor, finely chop the garlic and herbs. Add the onion and continue chopping. Add the crumbled stock cube and a liberal amount of seasoning.
3 Wash the bird inside and out, pat dry and fill with stuffing.
4 Rub thoroughly with olive oil, place on a rack in a roasting tin and roast for 45 minutes, basting occasionally with a mixture of the white wine and stock.

Meanwhile, prepare the peverada:
1 In a food processor, roughly mince the salami, livers, 1 garlic clove and the parsley. Transfer to a bowl and mix in the lemon zest and breadcrumbs.
2 In a frying pan, heat the olive oil – fry the remaining clove of garlic until brown then remove and discard it.
3 Add the salami mixture, stirring with a wooden spoon.
4 Moisten with a few drops of lemon juice and enough white wine to form a thick sauce.
5 Add a little salt and plenty of freshly ground black pepper – keep warm.

To serve:
1 Remove and discard the stuffing and cut the bird into serving pieces.
2 Arrange on heated plates with the sauce either spooned over or passed in a sauceboat.

INGREDIENTS

1 guinea fowl
extra virgin olive oil
120ml/4fl oz (½ cup) dry white
    wine
120ml/4fl oz (½ cup) good chicken
    stock

For the stuffing
2 cloves garlic
2 sprigs of fresh rosemary
1 sprig of fresh parsley
2 onions – roughly chopped
1 vegetable stock cube –
    crumbled
salt and freshly ground black
    pepper

For the peverada sauce
60g/2oz (⅓ cup) Italian salami,
    such as Soppressa
60g/2oz (⅓ cup) chicken livers
2 cloves garlic
1 sprig of fresh parsley
1 tsp grated lemon zest
30g/1oz (2 Tbl) breadcrumbs
1 Tbl extra virgin olive oil
a few drops of fresh lemon juice
dry white wine
salt and freshly ground black
    pepper

Serve with
polenta

Serves 2 to 3

Equipment
food processor
roasting tin/pan with rack

NOTES

Faraona con la Peverada (Italian)

Peverada is a descendant of peverata, a medieval Venetian sauce. The recipe often included anchovies, ginger and pomegranate juice. It is also served with hare that has been browned and simmered slowly with fried onions, garlic and stock until tender. In this case, the liver of the hare would be used to make the sauce and the reduced cooking juices also added to it.

Guinea fowl, descendant of a West African species, has been a prized eating bird in Italian cuisine since Roman times. Its flesh is a bit firmer than chicken with a touch of gamey flavour. Farmed guinea fowl are available all year round and can be prepared in any way suitable for chicken or pheasant.

SALMIS OF PHEASANT

....

CONTRIBUTED BY CHEF MARCUS TULLET
THE TURF CLUB, LONDON

Serves 4

Equipment
large, heavy roasting tin/pan

1 Preheat the oven to 220°C/425°F/Gas Mark 7.

2 In a large, heavy roasting tin, melt the lard and lightly brown the pheasants until sealed.

3 Add the garlic and vegetables and place in the oven, uncovered, for 10 minutes.

4 Remove the tin from the oven and reduce the oven temperature to 180°C/350°F/Gas Mark 4.

5 Sprinkle the flour into the tin and mix it thoroughly with the fat and vegetables. Add the brandy, wine, stock and herbs and cover with foil.

6 Return the birds to the oven to cook gently for a further 30 minutes. Remove them and allow to cool slightly.

7 Cut the legs and breasts from the carcasses and keep them warm and covered.

8 Roughly chop the carcasses and add the bones to the cooking stock. Boil gently for 15 minutes then pass through a sieve and season to taste.

9 Arrange the pheasant on very hot plates, coat with the sauce and serve immediately.

INGREDIENTS

2 large pheasants, prepared for
  cooking
15g/½ oz (1 Tbl) lard
1 clove garlic – finely chopped
1 stick celery – finely chopped
1 carrot – finely chopped
1 medium onion – finely chopped
1 small leek – finely chopped
30g/1oz (4 Tbl) plain/all purpose
  flour
60ml/2fl oz (¼ cup) brandy
385ml/13fl oz (1½ cups +
  2 Tbl) full-bodied red wine
300ml/10fl oz (1¼ cups) chicken
  stock
1 bay leaf
1 small sprig of thyme
salt and freshly ground black
  pepper to taste

NOTES

Be careful not to burn the pheasants or vegetables. If you have burnt bits in the roasting pan, the sauce will turn out bitter.

Pheasants, "the king of feathered game", were introduced to Europe from Asia in the Middle Ages and from there made their way to the Americas. The smaller hens are preferred to males for their finer flesh but both have a highly prized mild flavour. The age of a bird is critical when choosing a method of cooking. Young birds are best simply roasted, while older birds require longer cooking and more liquid. To tell the age of the bird, press the upper part of the beak and the area above the breastbone, both of which are pliable in young birds. With young birds, the long wing-tip feather is pointed, while in older birds it is rounded. Wild birds have more characteristic flavour, but the commonly available farmed variety are always plump and tender.

STUFFED BREAST OF PHEASANT AVYONA

CONTRIBUTED BY CHEF KEITH PODMORE
BOODLE'S, LONDON

INGREDIENTS

2 hen pheasants
vegetables in very fine matchsticks:
    45g/1½oz (¼ cup) carrot
    45g/1½oz (¼ cup) white of leek
    45g/1½oz (¼ cup) celery
60ml/2fl oz (¼ cup) dry white
    wine

For the stock/sauce
60g/2oz (½ cup) roughly chopped
    onion
60g/2oz (¼ cup) roughly chopped
    carrot
1 stick celery – roughly chopped
60g/2oz (½ cup) roughly chopped
    leek
1 bouquet garni
90g/3oz (6 Tbl) butter – in pieces

For the stuffing
1 Tbl chopped fresh parsley
1 Tbl chopped fresh chervil
1 Tbl snipped fresh chives
1 Tbl chopped fresh tarragon

salt and freshly ground black
    pepper to taste

To garnish
in very fine matchsticks:
    45g/1½oz (¼ cup) beetroot/beet
    45g/1½oz (¼ cup) mangetout/
    snow peas

Remove legs and breast supremes (skinned) from the
pheasants. Bone the thighs and reserve this meat for the
stuffing. Reserve the breast supremes.

Make the stock:
1 Place the pheasant legs, carcasses and bones in a large pan
with the stock ingredients – reserving the butter for later –
and 900ml/30fl oz (3¾ cups) cold water. Season lightly.
2 Bring to a rapid boil, skim any foam that rises, then lower
heat and simmer for 1½ hours.
3 Strain the stock, place in a clean saucepan and reduce until
slightly syrupy – set aside.

Prepare the dish:
1 Preheat the oven to 190°C/375°F/Gas Mark 5.
2 Finely mince the reserved thigh meat, mix with the stuffing
herbs and season to taste.
3 Cut a pocket in the side of the pheasant breasts and carefully
insert the stuffing. Refrigerate briefly (or for longer if
preparing in advance).
4 Season the buttered dish and sprinkle in the carrot, leek and
celery matchsticks.
5 Place the stuffed supremes on top, drizzle with wine and
season to taste. Place over a medium heat to warm, then cover
and place in the oven until done (approximately 15 minutes).
6 Transfer the supremes to a warm place. Drain any cooking
juices into the saucepan of reduced stock and reduce this sauce
further if necessary. Whisk the butter pieces into the sauce,
check the seasoning and keep warm.
7 Meanwhile, separately blanch the beetroot and mangetout.
8 Arrange the supremes on heated plates and scatter the
carrot, leek and celery over them.
9 Spoon the sauce over the pheasant, garnish with the
mangetout and beetroot matchsticks and serve immediately.

Serves 4

Equipment
Flame- and ovenproof dish with lid
    – buttered

NOTES

Bouquet garni is a bundle of
aromatic seasonings used to
flavour stocks and stews, usually
consisting of 2 or 3 sprigs of fresh
parsley, 2 bay leaves, a sprig of
thyme and anything else handy
and appropriate to the dish being
prepared, such as celery, leek,
savory, rosemary, sage, cloves,
dried citrus or peppercorns. Tie
together or enclose in a bit of
muslin for easy removal after
cooking.

PARSLIED CHICKEN WITH SHERRY VINEGAR SAUCE

CONTRIBUTED BY CHEF MICHEL GUÉRARD
LES PRÉS D'EUGÉNIE, EUGÉNIE LES BAINS, FRANCE

INGREDIENTS

1 x 1.4kg/3lb chicken
salt and freshly ground black
    pepper to taste

For the stuffing
50g/1¾oz (3½ Tbl) butter
1 rounded Tbl flat-leaf parsley –
    stalks removed
2 Tbl fresh lemon juice
1½ rounded tsp salt
4 grinds black pepper (¼ tsp)
50g/1¾oz (4 Tbl) fromage blanc
mirepoix: very finely chopped
    flat-leaf parsley (3 Tbl), chives
    (1 Tbl), tarragon (1 rounded
    tsp), shallots (2 rounded Tbl),
    5 button mushrooms, 50g/1¾oz
    (¼ cup) streaky bacon

For the sherry vinegar sauce
15g/½oz (1 Tbl) butter
1 rounded Tbl chopped shallots
2 Tbl sherry vinegar
3 Tbl chicken stock (or ⅒ stock
    cube dissolved in 3 Tbl hot
    water)
2 Tbl double/heavy cream
20g/¾oz (1½ Tbl) softened butter
    – in pieces
15g/½oz (1 Tbl) tomato pulp –
    finely chopped
1 rounded tsp chervil sprigs

To garnish
sprigs of flat-leaf parsley

Preheat the oven to 240°C/470°F/Gas Mark 9. Don't be put off by this high-temperature roasting technique – just be sure to baste frequently to produce a succulent and juicy bird.

Prepare the stuffing:
1 Place the butter, parsley, lemon juice, 1 Tbl water, salt and pepper in a food processor or blender and combine.
2 Transfer to a bowl. Add the fromage blanc and the mirepoix ingredients and combine with a fork to form a smooth stuffing.

Prepare the chicken:
1 By sliding your fingers slowly and very carefully between the skin and the flesh of the chicken, lift the skin away from the breast and thighs without tearing. Season the inside of the bird.
2 With your fingers, gently insert the stuffing between skin and flesh, patting it into an even layer over breast and thighs.
3 Roast the chicken on a rack, breast upwards, basting frequently, for 45 minutes, or until done (when a thin skewer inserted into the joint between drumstick and thigh produces clear juice without a rosy tinge).
4 Remove the chicken, place on a heated platter, cover with foil and keep warm.

Prepare the sherry vinegar sauce and serve:
1 Discard the fat from the roasting tin and replace it with the butter – place the tin over heat.
2 Add the shallots and sauté until softened but not browned.
3 Add the vinegar, scraping up all the caramelized roasting juices. Reduce the vinegar by ¾ of its volume.
4 Add the stock and cream, bring to the boil and reduce the liquid by ⅓. Beat in the butter pieces.
5 Strain through a wire sieve and add the tomato and chervil.
6 Cut the chicken into 4 pieces.
7 Cover 4 heated plates generously with sauce and arrange the chicken pieces on top – garnish with parsley and serve at once.

Serves 4

Equipment
food processor or blender
roasting tin/pan with rack

NOTES

The chicken can be prepared for the oven several hours in advance and refrigerated until needed. It should be at room temperature when placed in the oven.

Flat-leaf (Italian) parsley is similar to coriander in appearance. It has a better texture and a more complex and delicate flavour than curly-leaf parsley. Its ability to stand up to heat makes it preferable for cooking.

Chervil is an aromatic herb with a flavour similar to parsley but with a hint of anis. The fragile light-green lacy leaves wilt quickly after picking and long cooking destroys their delicate flavour. Chervil is said to intensify other herbs.

CHICKEN BREASTS WITH GINGER

CONTRIBUTED BY CAROLINE WALDEGRAVE, LONDON

Serves 4

1 Trim any excess fat from the chicken breasts.
2 In a large bowl, mix the onion, garlic, ginger, soy sauce, sherry, turmeric and cardamom seeds together.
3 Add the chicken breasts, coat well with the spice mixture, cover and refrigerate to marinate for anything from 30 minutes to 24 hours. (The longer the chicken marinates the better but just 30 minutes in the marinade will give it an excellent flavour.)
4 Preheat the oven to 180°C/350°F/Gas Mark 4.
5 Arrange a large sheet of foil in a flat baking dish and place the chicken breasts on top, making sure that they don't touch each other.
6 Pour the remaining marinade over the chicken. Fold up the foil to cover the chicken and seal the edges tightly, leaving room for air to circulate inside the parcel. Bake for 30 minutes.
7 Serve immediately on heated plates with the cooking juices spooned over as a sauce.

INGREDIENTS

4 chicken breasts – boned and
   skinned
1 small onion – finely chopped
2 cloves garlic – sliced
1 cm/½in piece of fresh ginger –
   peeled and finely chopped
2 Tbl light soy sauce
1 Tbl dry sherry
1 rounded tsp ground turmeric
seeds of 5 green cardamom pods

To garnish
a dusting of chopped fresh
   coriander/cilantro

Serve with
basmati rice or rice pilaf,
   cucumber raita, steamed
   broccoli and mango chutney

NOTES

Cardamom is an aromatic spice composed of small seeds encased in a dried pod. The most common type is green cardamom, so called because of the green/white colour of its pod, but there is also a larger, black variety, available in Indian markets. Cardamom loses its flavour very quickly and packaged ground cardamom is not recommended. Immediately before using this spice, break open the pods, remove the seeds and either grind them or use them whole.

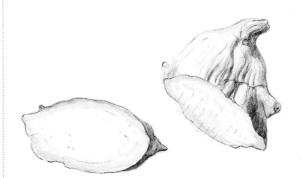

MUSTARD BBQ QUAIL WITH ONION AND BLACK-EYED PEA RELISH

CONTRIBUTED BY CHEF ELIZABETH B. TERRY
ELIZABETH ON 37TH, SAVANNAH, GEORGIA, USA

INGREDIENTS

12 quail – semi-boned

For the stuffing
225g/8oz spicy sausage meat/bulk
  sausage (Italian country style)
1 Vidalia onion – finely chopped
1 large Granny Smith apple –
  peeled, cored and finely chopped

For the onion relish
175g/6oz (1 cup) dried black-eyed
  peas – rinsed and drained
1 medium-sized sweet potato –
  peeled and diced
4 Tbl extra virgin olive oil
2 Vidalia onions — finely chopped
4 Tbl diced red bell pepper
4 Tbl shredded flat-leaf parsley
2 Tbl shredded basil
2 Tbl snipped fresh chives
2 Tbl raspberry vinegar
salt and freshly cracked black
  peppercorns to taste

For the mustard BBQ sauce
3 cloves garlic – finely chopped
½ tsp salt
2 tsp cracked black peppercorns
4 Tbl coarse mustard
2 Tbl Teriyaki sauce
4 Tbl chopped fresh thyme
1 tsp finely chopped lemon peel
4 Tbl fresh lemon juice
120ml/4fl oz (½ cup)
  groundnut/peanut oil

Prepare the stuffing:
1 In a medium frying pan, briefly sauté the sausage and onion. Stir constantly to break up the sausage and to avoid browning.
2 Add the apple and immediately drain away the fat from the sausage.
3 Cool, then chill – reserve.

Prepare the relish:
1 In a large bowl, cover the black-eyed peas with warm water and soak for 1 hour, then rinse carefully and drain.
2 Place the peas in a saucepan and cover with water. Add the diced sweet potato and a dash of salt, bring to the boil and skim off any foam that rises to the top.
3 Lower the heat and gently simmer for 15 minutes or until the peas and potatoes are tender – drain and set aside to cool.
4 In a frying pan, heat the olive oil. Add the onion, sauté over medium heat until transparent, then set aside to cool.
5 In a bowl, combine all the ingredients – reserve at room temperature.

Prepare the mustard BBQ sauce:
1 Place all ingredients except the oil in a food processor or blender.
2 With the motor running, slowly add the oil (the sauce will thicken) – reserve.

Cook and serve the quail:
1 Preheat the oven to 200°C/400°F/Gas Mark 6.
2 Check the quail to remove any missed bones in the cavities then stuff each one with the chilled stuffing mixture.
3 Arrange in a roasting tin, top with the BBQ sauce and roast until golden (approximately 20 minutes).
4 Divide the relish among 6 plates. Arrange 2 quail on each plate and serve at once.

Serves 6

Equipment
food processor or blender

NOTES

Serves 12 as a starter.

Quail, once a popular game bird, is available today farmed and has a delicate, only slightly gamey flavour. Because quail fly little, they do not have the strongly flavoured dark meat of other game birds.

Serve with roasted corn on the cob. Take each cob, pull down the outer husks, remove and discard the silk and pull the husks back around the corn. Soak in water for at least 15 minutes then place on a barbecue for 15 to 20 minutes or in a 200°C/400°F/Gas Mark 6 oven for 20 to 30 minutes. Turn occasionally, until tender and fragrant.

CHICKEN HASH

....

CONTRIBUTED BY CHEF M. J. HASLER
MARK'S CLUB, LONDON

INGREDIENTS

1 x 1.4kg/3lb cold roast chicken
   (reserve cooking fat from
   roasting tin)
1 Tbl Worcestershire sauce
300ml/10fl oz (1¼ cups)
   single/light cream
150ml/5fl oz (½ cup + 2 Tbl)
   double/heavy cream
3 egg yolks
4 slices of back bacon – very well
   grilled and chopped
salt and freshly ground black
   pepper to taste

To garnish
chopped fresh parsley
croûtons made from 2 slices of
   white bread, cut into heart
   shapes and fried golden brown

Serve with
basmati rice or rice pilaf and a
   mixed salad

1 Remove the drumsticks from the chicken and put aside for another use.
2 Remove all remaining flesh from the carcass, discarding the skin, excess fat and bones, and roughly chop the meat.
3 Preheat the oven grill/broiler.
4 In a large frying pan, melt the chicken fat reserved from the roasting tin.
5 When the fat sizzles, add the chicken, Worcestershire sauce and salt and pepper to taste, and stir for 2 minutes.
6 Add the single cream and bring to the boil, then lower the heat and simmer for 10 minutes until thickened.
7 In a bowl, whip the double cream and fold in the egg yolks.
8 Place the chicken mixture in a flameproof serving dish and sprinkle with bacon. Spread the whipped cream thinly over the top and place under the grill to brown.
9 Garnish with heart-shaped croûtons, sprinkle with parsley and serve piping hot on heated plates.

Serves 4

Equipment
oven grill/broiler
flameproof serving dish

NOTES

Do not freeze this dish.

Bacon is cured meat from the back or side of the pig. "Green" bacon has been cured either in brine or with salt and spices. "Smoked" bacon is green bacon further treated with a smoking process to give it a more intense flavour. There are a wide variety of cuts available in Great Britain while in the US "bacon" almost always refers to smoked streaky bacon. Back bacons are meaty rashers/slices for grilling or frying with a variety of names indicating the particular cut from which they were taken – Canadian Bacon is the closest substitute in the US market.

CHICKEN ISOLABELLA

CONTRIBUTED BY CHEF SATISH DESIGAR
THE ARMY AND NAVY CLUB, LONDON

1 Prepare the forcemeat by processing all the ingredients in a food processor or blender until smooth.

2 Remove small fillets from the inside of each chicken breast. Flatten out the breasts and fillets by placing between 2 sheets of strong greaseproof paper and gently pounding with a heavy implement.

3 Place quarter of the forcemeat in the middle of each breast and cover with a fillet. Fold the breasts up over the fillets to enclose the stuffing and season each parcel.

4 In a frying pan, melt the butter. Gently place the parcels seam-side down in the pan, let them take a golden colour, then carefully turn.

5 When the chicken is golden all over, pour in the wine and stock. Add the mushrooms, cover and cook gently for 15–20 minutes, turning 2 or 3 times.

6 Transfer the chicken to a hot serving dish, top with the mushrooms and keep warm.

7 Return the frying pan to high heat and reduce the cooking liquid to 2–3 Tbl.

8 In a small bowl, blend together the butter and flour to make the beurre manié. Add the milk and cream to the frying pan, and whisk in enough beurre manié to thicken the sauce. Beat vigorously until it reaches the boil.

9 Whisk in the Calvados and let boil for 1 or 2 minutes. Check seasoning, then pour over the chicken breasts. Serve at once.

Serves 4

Equipment
food processor or blender
greased paper/waxed paper

NOTES

Suprême de Volaille Isolabella (French)

The chicken parcels may be made in advance and refrigerated for several hours before final cooking

Cèpes/ceps/porcini (Boletus edulis) are flavourful and highly prized wild mushrooms with bulbous stalks and fleshy brownish caps underneath which are tiny tubes (instead of the more common gills). Often found dried in speciality shops, fresh ones can be difficult to locate. If unavailable, other types of wild or cultivated mushroom may be substituted.

INGREDIENTS

4 chicken breasts – boned, wings
    and skin removed
120g/4oz (8 Tbl) unsalted butter
90ml/3fl oz (6 Tbl) dry white wine
500ml/17fl oz (2 cups + 2 Tbl)
    good chicken stock
225g/8oz (2 cups) fresh
    cèpes/ceps/porcini mushrooms
    – sliced
salt and freshly ground white
    pepper to taste

For the forcemeat
255g/9oz uncooked scampi/large
    shrimp – peeled, deveined and
    chopped
1 egg white
3 Tbl double/heavy cream
salt and freshly ground white
    pepper to taste

For the sauce
beurre manié: 120g/4oz (8 Tbl)
    unsalted butter and 60g/2oz
    (½ cup) sifted plain/all purpose
    flour
265ml/9fl oz (1 cup + 2 Tbl) fresh
    rich milk
265ml/9fl oz (1 cup + 2 Tbl)
    double/heavy cream
4 Tbl Calvados

Serve with
wild rice and green salad

85

ROAST SNIPE WITH BRAISED CABBAGE

....

CONTRIBUTED BY CHEF NEIL PASS
RULES, LONDON

INGREDIENTS

2 snipe – heads and feathers
   removed but innards kept in
a pinch of plain/all purpose flour
1 large croûton

For the gravy
45g/1½oz (3 Tbl) butter
1 onion – finely diced
1 carrot – finely diced
1 stick of celery – finely diced
white part of a leek – finely diced
pinch of fresh thyme
2 Tbl red wine vinegar
120ml/4fl oz (½ cup) red wine
120ml/4fl oz (½ cup) game stock
120ml/4fl oz (½ cup) veal stock
1 tsp redcurrant jelly

For the braised cabbage
30g/1oz (2 Tbl) butter
1 onion – finely sliced
120g/4oz smoked streaky bacon –
   in julienne strips
¼ Savoy cabbage – finely sliced
600ml/1 pint (2½ cups) game stock

salt and freshly ground black
   pepper to taste

For the garnish
1 potato cut into matchsticks
oil for deep-frying
small sprig of fresh watercress

Preheat the oven to 240°C/450°F/Gas Mark 8. Season the birds well (no need to lard them as they are cooked quickly) and sprinkle lightly with flour (to prevent drying out).

Prepare the gravy:
1 In a saucepan, heat 30g/1oz (2 Tbl) of the butter.
2 Add the onion, carrot, celery, leek and thyme and gently sauté until lightly browned.
3 Deglaze with vinegar until evaporated.
4 Add the red wine and reduce until a syrup. Add game and veal stocks and reduce approximately by half.
5 Finish the gravy with the redcurrant jelly. Just before serving, whisk in the remaining 15g/½oz (1 Tbl) butter and taste and correct seasoning.

Prepare and serve the dish:
1 Roast the birds for 12 minutes. When cooked (slightly pink inside), remove from oven, cover and let rest for 5 minutes.
2 Prepare the cabbage: in a casserole, heat the butter, sauté the onion and bacon pieces until brown, then add the cabbage and stock. Season well, cover and place in the oven until the liquid has evaporated.
3 Prepare the garnish: deep-fry the potato matchsticks until golden brown (to make game chips).
4 Place the warm croûton in the middle of a heated serving plate and scrape the innards from the birds on to the croûton. Place the birds on top.
5 Arrange braised cabbage and game chips on the plate, garnish with a small sprig of watercress and serve immediately, passing gravy separately.

Servings: 2 birds per person

Equipment
flame- and ovenproof casserole

NOTES

Snipe are migratory game birds smaller than but similar to the woodcock. Best in the autumn, they are rare and highly prized. Woodcock, an even more difficult bird to obtain, is the only real substitute. This recipe is delicious with other small game or quality free-range birds (such as partridge or quail). Simply adjust cooking time accordingly to the size of the bird. (Game birds are done once the juices run pink when the flesh is pierced.)

To make the croûton for this dish, sauté a crustless round of bread in clarified butter until golden brown.

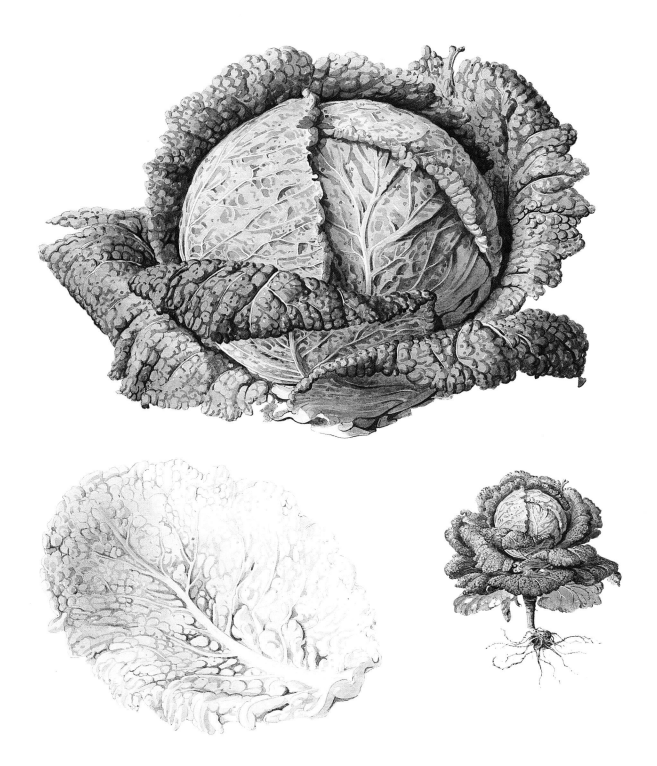

CHICKEN ROMANCE

....

CONTRIBUTED BY AZIZA'S RESTAURANT, SINGAPORE

INGREDIENTS

....

4 chicken pieces, ideally breasts on
  the bone with skin intact
4 Tbl honey
4 small aubergines/eggplants
non-scented oil for deep-frying

For the sauce
300ml/10fl oz (1¼ cups) thick
  coconut milk
2 cloves garlic – finely chopped
2 shallots (small purple Asian or
  larger brown French) – finely
  chopped
a pinch freshly ground black
  pepper or 1 tsp chilli powder
2 bay leaves
1 Tbl fresh lime juice
1 stalk lemongrass finely sliced and
  bruised
salt to taste

To garnish
wedges of fresh lime
sprigs of fresh coriander/cilantro

Serve with
white rice

1 Preheat the grill/broiler, grill pan or barbecue.
2 Rub the chicken with the honey.
3 Place all the sauce ingredients in a heavy-bottomed saucepan and simmer for 10 minutes (do not allow sauce to bubble).
4 In a wok or deep pan, heat enough oil to deep-fry the aubergines.
5 Place the chicken on or under the grill and cook gently until golden brown and just cooked through.
6 As the chicken is grilling, make four lengthways cuts in the aubergines (leaving them connected at the top) and rub with salt. Deep-fry the aubergine "fans" until brown – drain on kitchen paper and keep warm.

Assemble the dish on heated plates:
1 Flatten the grilled chicken with the back of a broad knife.
2 Place a piece of chicken in the centre of each plate and "crown" with an aubergine fan.
3 Remove the bay leaves from the sauce. Generously coat the dish with the sauce.
4 Garnish with lime wedges and coriander and serve at once.

Serves 4

Equipment
grill/broiler, grill pan or barbecue
wok or deep pan

NOTES

Ayam Pecel Asmara (Indonesian)

Coconut milk (in tins, bottles and boxes) is widely available in all Asian markets and many supermarkets. It is not the liquid found inside coconuts but rather a creamy substance extracted by squeezing the shredded meat of the nut. Coconut milk from a box or bottle is best for this recipe, because that from a tin can be a little too creamy.

SOUFFLÉ INDIENNE

CONTRIBUTED BY CHEF JUDY MARJORIBANKS
THE COMPLEAT KITCHEN, GLOUCESTERSHIRE, ENGLAND

Serves 6 to 8

Equipment
a 25 × 35cm/10 × 14in nonstick
    Swiss/jelly-roll tin/pan — lined
    with parchment paper that is
    greased with clarified butter

NOTES

This dish can be prepared ahead
of time and reheated just before
serving; it can also be frozen. It
serves 10 to 12 as a starter.

Mint chutney makes an excellent
accompaniment. Take 60g/2oz (1¾
cups) fresh mint leaves, 4 Tbl
finely chopped onion, 2 tsp finely
chopped seeded green chillies,
1 tsp finely chopped fresh ginger
and 2 tsp caster/superfine sugar
and combine in a food processor
or blender. Slowly add 4 Tbl cider
vinegar, then pour into a bowl,
cover and refrigerate until needed
(up to 2 days).

Prepare the soufflé roll:
1 Preheat the oven to 180°C/350°F/Gas Mark 4.
2 In a medium saucepan, melt the butter. Add the flour and
paprika and cook, stirring constantly, for 2 minutes.
3 Pour in the hot milk and whisk until smooth and thickened.
Season with the salt and remove from heat.
4 One at a time, whisk in the egg yolks.
5 In a clean, dry bowl, beat the egg whites until stiff but not
dry and then fold into the mixture.
6 Spread over the base of the prepared tin and bake for
approximately 20 minutes, until puffed and golden.

Prepare the filling:
1 In a saucepan, melt the butter. Stir in the curry powder and
flour and blend well.
2 Gradually add the stock and blend until smooth. Season with
lemon juice, salt and freshly ground pepper, then stir in the
chicken, red pepper and coriander.
3 Add the cream, heat through and reserve.

Assemble and serve the dish:
1 Remove the soufflé from the oven, turn out on to a damp
cloth and allow to cool for a few minutes.
2 Spread the filling evenly over the base.
3 Using the cloth for help, roll up the soufflé like a Swiss roll
and carefully transfer it back to the baking tin.
4 Brush with melted butter and bake until golden: 10 minutes.
5 Serve immediately on heated plates. If desired, garnish with a
little mint chutney (see Notes) and pass the remainder
separately.

INGREDIENTS

For the soufflé roll
30g/1oz (2 Tbl) unsalted butter
30g/1oz (4 Tbl) plain/all purpose
    flour
¾ tsp sweet paprika
265ml/9fl oz (1 cup + 2 Tbl) milk
    – scalded
¾ tsp salt
5 eggs – separated
additional melted butter

For the filling
30g/1oz (2 Tbl) unsalted butter
1 Tbl medium curry powder
30g/1oz (4 Tbl) plain/all purpose
    flour
200ml/6½ fl oz (¾ cup + 1 Tbl)
    chicken stock
1 tsp fresh lemon juice
salt and freshly ground black
    pepper to taste
175g/6oz (1 cup) cooked
    chopped chicken (1 breast)
60g/2oz (½ cup) finely chopped
    red bell pepper
60g/2oz (1¾ cups) chopped fresh
    coriander/cilantro leaves
4 Tbl double/heavy cream

MEAT

GRILLED FOIE GRAS AND PEARS

CONTRIBUTED BY CHEF KEVIN GRAHAM
WINDSOR COURT HOTEL, NEW ORLEANS, LOUISIANA, USA

INGREDIENTS

120ml/4fl oz (½ cup) Poire William liqueur (or other pear-flavoured liqueur)

235ml/8fl oz (1 cup) dry white wine

2 ripe pears – peeled, quartered and cored

1 x 680g/1½ lb uncooked whole "foie gras" duck liver

salt and freshly ground black pepper to taste

Serve with
a lightly dressed green salad

1 In a shallow glass or ceramic dish combine the Poire William and wine – set aside.

2 Slice the pear quarters into fans by cutting lengthways into slices, almost but not quite through to the stem end. The stem end will hold the fans together.

3 Place the pear fans in the wine mixture and marinate at room temperature for 1 hour.

4 Light the grill/barbecue.

5 Pull apart the two lobes of the duck liver. Starting from the thin end of each lobe, cut diagonally into 8 x 1cm/⅓in thick slices and season lightly with salt and pepper to taste.

6 When the grill is red hot, remove the pears from the marinade and lay them flat on the hottest part of the grill to score. Turn and move off to the side of the grill. Baste with marinade and grill until tender (approximately 3–4 mins).

7 Meanwhile arrange the liver slices over the hottest part of the grill, score on both sides, then baste with the marinade and grill for 30 seconds.

8 Immediately remove the liver slices from the grill, arrange on warm serving plates with the pear fans (with the duck liver at the base of the fanned pear), drizzle a little of the marinade on to each plate and serve immediately.

Serves 4

Equipment
charcoal or gas grill/barbecue
shallow glass or ceramic dish

NOTES

Serves 8 as a starter.

Poire William, a famous eau de vie, is a pear-based white brandy. Eaux de vie are fruit- or herb-based spirits, differing from the more widely know brandy by being unsweetened and aged in glass rather than wooden containers.

Foie gras ("fat liver"), obtained from either ducks or geese, is the enlarged liver resulting from the methodical feeding and fattening of the birds. Considered a rare delicacy, the uncooked version is available on special order from quality butchers.

ROGNONS CHEZ MOI

CONTRIBUTED BY THE VISCOUNTESS PORTMAN, HEREFORDSHIRE, ENGLAND

Serves 2

1 Prepare the kidneys by removing any outer membranes, cutting into quarters and trimming away the central core of fat together with any large blood vessels.

2 Dust the kidney pieces with flour seasoned generously with salt and pepper. Shake off any excess coating and reserve the seasoned flour.

3 Heat the butter in a frying pan and, when it stops foaming, sauté the kidneys gently until browned – be careful not to cook through at this stage.

4 Add the reserved flour, the mustard, stock and wine and stir, scraping the pan bottom to deglaze and incorporate any caramelized cooking juices into the sauce.

5 Cook until kidneys are just done – do not overcook.

6 Add the cream, check and adjust the seasoning.

7 Place on heated plates, sprinkle with chopped parsley and serve at once.

INGREDIENTS

450g/1lb lamb kidneys
1 rounded Tbl plain/all purpose flour
30g/1oz (2 Tbl) butter
3 rounded tsp Dijon mustard or to taste
90ml/3fl oz (6 Tbl) veal or chicken stock
1 Tbl red wine
4 Tbl single/light cream
salt and freshly ground black pepper to taste

To garnish
a dusting of chopped fresh parsley

Serve
simply on toast, or for a more substantial meal with sautéed or mashed potatoes, a green salad and warm crusty bread

NOTES

Veal kidneys may be substituted.

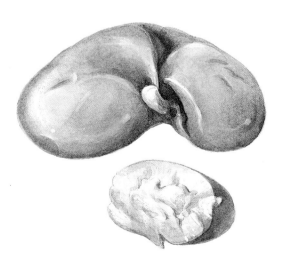

FILLET OF KENT LAMB WITH FRESH MINT CREAM SAUCE

CONTRIBUTED BY CHEF MARJAN LESNIK
CLARIDGE'S, LONDON

INGREDIENTS

4 pairs best end of Kent Spring
    lamb
2 Tbl non-scented oil
120g/4oz (8 Tbl) unsalted butter
90g/3oz (½ cup) chopped shallots
1 bunch mint – roughly chopped
180ml/6fl oz (¾ cup) dry white
    wine
300ml/10fl oz (1¼ cups) fond
    d'agneau lié/thickened lamb
    stock
300ml/10fl oz (1¼ cups)
    double/heavy cream
salt and freshly ground black
    pepper to taste

To garnish
8 mint leaves

Serve with
potato snow

Serves 8

Equipment
fine sieve/chinois

1 Remove the eye of the meat from the best ends and trim all sinews and excess meat. Roughly chop and reserve some of the best trimmings for enriching the sauce (use the remaining trimmings and the bones to make stock). Most butchers will do this on request.

2 In a large frying pan, heat the oil and seal the fillets on all sides, cooking until just pink. Remove the meat and place on a rack in a clean pan to allow any juices to drain – keep warm.

3 Discard the oil from the pan, add half the butter, the reserved meat trimmings, the shallots and half the mint. Cover and leave to soften over low heat without colouring.

4 Add the white wine and reduce to a syrup-like consistency.

5 Add the fond d'agneau lié and reduce the brown mint sauce to the desired consistency and peak of flavour. Strain three-quarters of it into a clean saucepan — cover and keep warm.

6 Return the frying pan to the heat and reduce by half or until it coats the back of a metal spoon. Add the cream and remaining mint and gently simmer the sauce to infuse the cream with the mint.

7 Taste and add seasoning then strain the cream sauce through a fine sieve into a clean saucepan and whisk in the remaining butter. Coat heated serving plates with the cream sauce.

8 Slice the fillets thinly at an angle and arrange in a fan on top of the cream sauce.

9 Add meat drippings to the brown mint sauce and spoon over the sliced lamb. Garnish with mint leaves and serve at once.

NOTES

Filet d'Agneau de Lait du Kent Poêlé, Sauce à la Crème de Menthe Fraîche (French)

To prepare potato snow, scoop out the contents of freshly baked potatoes (preferably the King Edward variety). Immediately rice the potato into a warmed, fancy-folded napkin and serve.

Loin of Lamb with Vegetable Ragoût and Gingered Couscous

CONTRIBUTED BY CHEF STEPHAN PYLES, DALLAS, TEXAS, USA

INGREDIENTS

For the vegetable ragoût
5 medium tomatoes
120ml/4fl oz (8 Tbl) olive oil
75g/2½oz (½ cup) peeled
    aubergine/eggplant in 6mm/¼in
    dice
120g/4oz (½ cup) onions in
    6mm/¼in dice
75g/2½oz (½ cup) courgette/
    zucchini in 6mm/¼in dice
2 Tbl finely chopped garlic
1 Tbl chopped fresh thyme
1 Tbl chopped fresh oregano
2 Tbl tomato paste/purée
4 Tbl chopped fresh basil
4 Tbl chopped fresh parsley
salt and freshly ground black
    pepper to taste

Continued opposite

Prepare the ragoût:

1 Peel, seed and cut the tomatoes into 6mm/¼in dice and place in a strainer set over a bowl to drain – set aside.

2 In a large frying pan, heat half the oil until lightly smoking.

3 Add the aubergine, salt lightly and sauté for 5 minutes, stirring frequently (aubergine should be translucent).

4 Place the aubergine in a colander over a bowl and weigh down with a plate to drain off the bitter juices and excess oil – set aside.

5 In the same pan, heat the remaining oil until lightly smoking.

6 Add the onion and courgette and sauté for 2 minutes.

7 Add the tomatoes, garlic, thyme, oregano and tomato paste and cook over high heat, stirring frequently, until all the liquid has evaporated (approximately 10–15 minutes).

8 Stir in the basil, parsley and aubergine and continue cooking for 2 minutes.

9 Season with salt and freshly ground black pepper – reserve and keep warm.

Serves 4

NOTES

Adapted from
The New Texas Cuisine,
Doubleday, 1993.

Meanwhile, prepare the couscous:

1 In a saucepan, bring the chicken stock to the boil.

2 Add the ginger, turn off the heat and allow to steep for 15 minutes.

3 Strain to remove and discard the ginger and return the broth to the saucepan.

4 Add the salt and cinnamon and return to the boil.

5 All at once, add the couscous. Stir until all the liquid is absorbed.

6 Remove from the heat and, with a fork, gradually incorporate the butter, breaking up any lumps.

7 Add the crystallized ginger, tomato and apricot and combine thoroughly – set aside. (It can be reheated in a little chicken stock and butter.) Prepare the loin of lamb and serve the dish – see overleaf.

INGREDIENTS

For the gingered couscous
180ml/6fl oz (¾ cup) chicken stock
2 Tbl peeled and chopped fresh ginger
1 tsp salt
½ tsp ground cinnamon
225g/8oz (1 cup) couscous
60g/2oz (4 Tbl) unsalted butter
2 Tbl minced crystallized ginger
1 Tbl finely chopped tomato
1 Tbl finely diced dried apricot

Continued overleaf

INGREDIENTS

....

For the loin of lamb
2 boned and trimmed loins of
   lamb (bones reserved for stock)
3 Tbl olive oil
½ sweet onion, preferably Vidalia
   – chopped
¼ carrot – chopped
¼ celery stick – chopped
120ml/4fl oz (½ cup) dry red wine
180ml/6fl oz (¾ cup) reduced
   lamb or veal stock
1 tsp freshly ground cumin seeds
3 serrano chillies – cut in half
2 sprigs fresh thyme
2 sprigs fresh rosemary
30g/1oz (2 Tbl) butter
salt to taste

To garnish
sprigs of fresh rosemary and
   thyme

Meanwhile, prepare the lamb:

1 Preheat the oven to 180°C/350°F/Gas Mark 4.

2 Season the loins of lamb with salt.

3 In an ovenproof pan, heat 2 Tbl of the olive oil over high heat.

4 Add the loins, sear on all sides and remove – reserve.

5 In the same pan, heat the remaining oil. Add the onion, carrot and celery and cook for approximately 2 minutes.

6 Return the loins to the pan and place in the oven for 10–15 minutes until medium-rare.

7 Remove from the oven and place the loins on a warmed plate. Cover and allow to rest while finishing the sauce.

8 Return the pan to high heat, add the red wine and reduce to a glaze.

9 Lower the heat and add the stock, cumin, chillies, thyme and rosemary. Simmer for 5 minutes (for a spicier sauce, allow the chillies to steep longer).

10 Whisk the butter into the sauce, season with salt to taste and strain.

Assemble the dish:

1 Cut the loins into thick slices (1cm/⅓in or slightly thicker).

2 Cover the bottom of 4 heated dinner plates with the sauce.

3 Arrange a mound of couscous in centre of each plate.

4 Arrange the sliced meat on the sauce, interspacing it with spoonfuls of the vegetable ragoût.

5 Garnish plates with sprigs of fresh rosemary and thyme.

6 Serve immediately.

NOTES

Vidalia onions are large sweet onions particular to the southeastern United States. They are sometimes available in gourmet stores. Sweet Maui onions from Hawaii are perhaps the best substitute, but the more common Bermuda or Spanish onions could be used although their taste is noticeably sharper.

Serrano/Spanish (mountain) chillies are one of the hottest chillies commonly available. They are cylindrical (about 5cm/2in long and 6mm/¼in around) and can be bright green or red. Serrano are available in many supermarkets and are also found pickled and dried. Other types of fresh hot chillies can be substituted: because all chillies, even of the same species, vary in "hotness", taste the sauce frequently to achieve the degree of "heat" preferred and remove the chillies at that point.

SAUTÉED LAMB WITH CRAYFISH

CONTRIBUTED BY CHEF ALAIN SENDERENS
LUCAS CARTON, PARIS, FRANCE

1 Remove the sand track from the écrevisses: holding the body, twist the tail a quarter turn. Using a cocktail stick, gently pick up, extract and discard the long black filament in a single piece. Rinse, drain and reserve the cleaned écrevisses.

2 In a sauté pan, heat the peanut oil over high heat. Season the lamb, add to the pan and brown until golden: 5 to 6 minutes.

3 Add the butter, carrots and onion and simmer for 3 minutes.

4 Remove and reserve the lamb pieces. Drain and discard the grease from the vegetables, then purée the vegetables and reserve them.

INGREDIENTS

24 uncooked écrevisses/crayfish
1 Tbl groundnut/peanut oil
800g/1¾ lb shoulder of lamb – cut into 3cm/1¼in cubes
15g/½oz (1 Tbl) butter
120g/4oz (½ cup) finely diced carrots
60g/2oz (½ cup) finely diced onion
1 Tbl olive oil
4 Tbl cognac
255g/9oz (1¼ cups) tomatoes – peeled, seeded and diced
3 cloves garlic – finely minced
1 bouquet garni: 1 bay leaf, 3 sprigs of parsley, 1 sprig of thyme tied in a piece of muslin
1 tsp beef essence (see Notes)
400ml/14fl oz (1¾ cups) water
1 tsp coarse sea salt
salt and freshly ground black pepper

Serves 4

Equipment
food mill or processor
fine sieve/chinois

NOTES

Sauté d'Agneau aux Ecrevisses (French)

This dish can also be made with chicken instead of lamb.

Ecrevisses/crayfish are freshwater crustaceans that resemble tiny lobsters. Highly prized for their flavour, they are available worldwide both live and frozen. The sand tract may be removed while the creatures are still live, but care must be taken to avoid the tiny claws. They are particularly popular in Louisiana where they are called "crawfish", "yabbies" or "mudbugs" and enthusiastically eaten in large quantities simply boiled with a hot spice mixture.

5 Wipe the pan clean, add the olive oil and return to high heat. Add the écrevisses, sauté until pink, then remove and drain.

6 Wipe the pan clean, return the lamb and onion/carrot purée to it and place over medium heat. Pour in the cognac and heat for 2 minutes. Stir in the tomatoes, garlic and bouquet garni and cook for 5 minutes.

7 Meanwhile, remove the heads from the écrevisses and add the heads (reserving 4 to garnish the final presentation) to the lamb. Shell the tails and place the meat in a clean pan. Set aside.

8 Add the beef essence, water, coarse sea salt and 6 turns of pepper to the lamb. Cover and reduce the heat to low. Simmer for 45 minutes, stirring occasionally.

9 Remove the lamb pieces and place in the saucepan with the reserved tail meat. Place a fine sieve over this pan and strain the pan juices over the lamb and the tail meat, pressing down firmly to extract the flavour from the shells of the écrevisses. Heat the dish through.

10 Arrange on a heated serving plate, garnish with the 4 reserved heads and serve at once.

Beef essence is concentrated beef stock. In a heavy-bottomed saucepan, bring any stock to the boil. Reduce by at least three-quarters until it is thick and creamy, skimming if necessary. Store in small portions in the freezer and use sparingly. A beef bouillon cube will do here if necessary instead of the teaspoon of beef essence.

ROAST SHOULDER OF LAMB

CONTRIBUTED BY LA GAZELLE D'OR
TAROUDANT, MOROCCO

INGREDIENTS

1.4–1.6kg/3–3½ lb new season
shoulder of lamb, as lean as
possible – either boned and
rolled or whole
½ tsp ground cumin
½ tsp ground dried ginger
2 tsp sweet paprika
a few strands of saffron
½ tsp freshly ground white pepper
salt to taste
150–200g/5–7oz butter
(depending on leanness of
meat)
2 medium onions – sliced
3 cloves garlic – finely chopped

Serve with
wild rice or pommes noisette with
french beans or mangetout

1 Wash the lamb and pat dry.

2 In a small bowl, combine the cumin, ginger, paprika, saffron, white pepper and salt. Rub this spice mixture into the lamb.

3 Place the lamb in a heavy saucepan and half cover with water. Add the butter, onion and garlic and bring to the boil.

4 Reduce the heat, cover and simmer, turning the meat occasionally, for 1½ to 2 hours until the meat is tender. The sauce should be thick by now – partially uncover the pan if necessary to reduce it.

5 Near the end of the cooking time, preheat the oven to 220°C/425°F/Gas Mark 7.

6 Remove the lamb from the sauce and place in an ovenproof dish in the hot oven to brown for 20 minutes.

7 Meanwhile, keep the sauce warm, simmering to reduce it further if necessary.

8 Arrange the meat on a warmed serving platter. Pour some of the warm sauce over it, reserving the rest to serve on the side of each plate, and serve at once.

Serves 6

Equipment
heavy saucepan with lid
ovenproof dish

NOTES

Cumin is a small dried seed (available in white, brown and black varieties) with a very distinctive earthy and aromatic flavour. An essential component of Middle Eastern, north African and central American cuisines, it also appears in European bread and cheese recipes. Use in small amounts, whole or freshly ground, to add an exotic richness to many dishes.

Dried ginger is a powdered spice, valued since the Middle Ages for its distinctive pungent sweet–hot flavour. While it is the result of drying and grinding ginger root, it is definitely not an acceptable substitute in recipes calling for fresh ginger root.

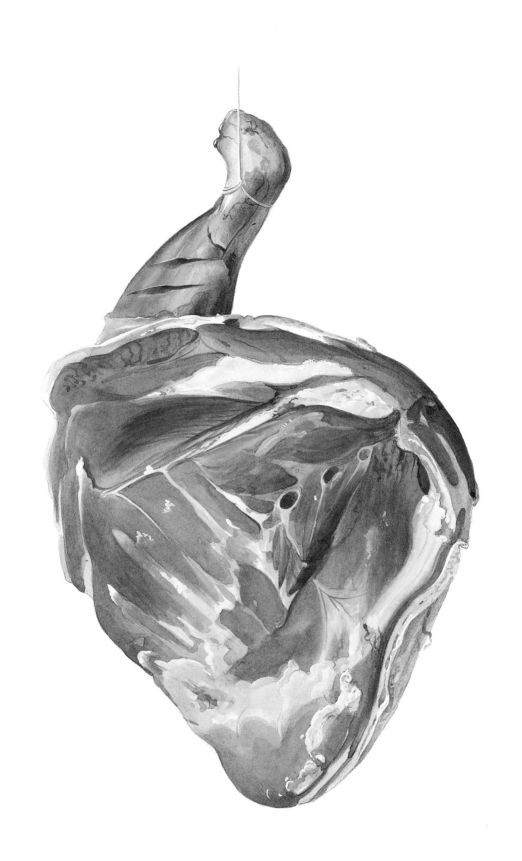

SHOULDER OF LAMB WITH FETA CHEESE AND TOMATO MINT SALSA

CONTRIBUTED BY FIONA BURRELL, CO-PRINCIPAL
LEITH'S SCHOOL OF FOOD AND WINE, LONDON

INGREDIENTS

1 shoulder of lamb – boned
(approximately 1.8kg/4lb after
boning)
6 Tbl red wine
6 Tbl plain/all purpose flour

For the stuffing
225g/8oz (1½ cups) feta cheese –
cut into 1cm/½in cubes
2 rounded tsp green peppercorns
1 shallot – chopped
90g/3oz (1½ cups) fresh
breadcrumbs
2 Tbl thinly sliced sundried
tomatoes
1 rounded Tbl fresh thyme leaves
1 egg, beaten
salt and freshly ground black
pepper to taste

For the tomato mint salsa
1 shallot – finely diced
1 Tbl red wine vinegar
3 Tbl extra virgin olive oil
4 tomatoes – peeled, seeded and
chopped
1 clove garlic – finely chopped
1 rounded Tbl chopped fresh mint
salt and freshly ground black
pepper to taste

To garnish
sprigs of fresh mint

Prepare the lamb:

1 Preheat the oven to 200°C/400°F/Gas Mark 6.

2 Trim the lamb of excess fat, leaving a thin layer on the
outside.

3 Mix all the stuffing ingredients together, beat lightly and
season. Season the inside of the lamb and stuff it carefully.
Using a trussing needle and thin kitchen string, sew the lamb
up – not too tightly.

4 Weigh the lamb and calculate cooking time: for pink lamb
allow 20 minutes per 450g/1 lb; for better done lamb cook a
further 30 minutes.

5 Place the lamb in a roasting tin and into the oven.

6 Thirty minutes before the lamb is ready, pour the red wine
over it.

Meanwhile, prepare the tomato mint salsa:

1 Mix the shallot, vinegar and oil together – stand for 10
minutes.

2 Add the tomatoes, garlic and mint, and season with salt and
pepper. Set aside.

To serve:

1 When the lamb is done, place it on a heated platter – allow it
to rest, keeping it warm, for 10 minutes.

2 Pour off all but 1 Tbl of fat from the roasting tin. Place it on
the heat, add the flour and cook, stirring, for 1 minute.

3 Add any roasting juices from the platter and some water and
bring to the boil. Lower the heat and simmer the gravy for 5
minutes, then taste and season.

4 Just before serving, remove the string from the lamb.

5 Serve the lamb with the gravy, garnished with a sprig of fresh
mint, passing the tomato and mint salsa separately.

Serves 6

Equipment
trussing needle
thin kitchen string

NOTES

Roasts should always be at room
temperature before going into the
oven. It is also important to let
meat rest after roasting so that
the juices, which are driven to the
centre of the meat by the cooking
heat, return to the outside of the
roast. The meat relaxes, and
becomes more tender.

Welsh Mountain Lamb with Asparagus and Butternut Squash

CONTRIBUTED BY CHEF WENDY VAUGHAN
THE OLD RECTORY, CONWY, GWYNEDD, WALES

Prepare the lamb:

1 Preheat the oven to 240°C/475°F/Gas Mark 9.

2 In a bowl, combine the butter and thyme and add the salt and pepper. Rub the mixture all over the lamb.

3 Place in a roasting tin and roast for 15 to 20 minutes for pink lamb (well-done lamb takes longer), basting occasionally.

Meanwhile, prepare the sauce:

1 In a saucepan, melt 30g/1oz (2 Tbl) of the butter without browning.

2 Add the onion, cover and leave over low heat to soften without colouring, stirring occasionally.

3 Add the wine, raise heat and bring to the boil, uncovered. Reduce to 2 Tbl. Add the stock and reduce by half.

Finish the dish:

1 Add the squash balls to the sauce, simmer until tender and remove. Drain and keep warm.

2 Break off the tender asparagus tips (reserve the tougher stalks for vegetable stock or soup), steam until tender, drain and keep warm.

3 Finish the sauce by whisking in the remaining 30g/1oz (2 Tbl) of butter (cut into small pieces).

4 Slice the lamb into 2 or 3 thick slices per person. Arrange on heated plates, decorate with the vegetables, spoon the sauce over and serve at once.

Serves 4

Equipment
melon baller
vegetable steamer – optional

INGREDIENTS

60g/2oz (4 Tbl) unsalted butter
1 tsp chopped fresh thyme
2 x 340–400g/12–14oz fillets of Welsh lamb (or 2 boned loins) – trimmed
1 level tsp salt and freshly ground black pepper to taste

For the sauce
60g/2oz (4 Tbl) unsalted butter
1 small onion – finely chopped
120ml/4fl oz (½ cup) dry white wine
600ml/20fl oz (2½ cups) chicken stock

The vegetables
450g/1lb butternut squash – cut into small balls, using a melon baller
450g/1lb fresh green asparagus

NOTES

Asparagus comes in many types, roughly divided into four groups: green asparagus is the most flavourful and the one favoured by UK and US markets; white asparagus, grown in deep trenches blanketed with earth to prevent it ever appearing above ground, is valued for its very delicate flavour; purple asparagus, grown in deep trenches but harvested when several centimetres above ground, is similar to but more flavourful than the white variety; and wild asparagus, pencil-thin green shoots with a famous bitter taste, is traditionally hunted in early spring and quickly prepared with hard-boiled eggs and olive oil or butter.

Choose asparagus with firm straight stems and tightly closed buds. Store this delicacy as you would any flower: trim the end of the stem, place the stalks upright in water, cover loosely with a plastic bag and refrigerate.

LAMB MEDALLIONS WITH TEA LEAVES AND FRESH MINT

CONTRIBUTED BY CHEF CHRISTIAN BODIGUEL
VENICE SIMPLON-ORIENT-EXPRESS

INGREDIENTS

1kg/2lb 3oz saddle of lamb
(weight with bones in) – bones
removed and reserved for
sauce

2 Tbl groundnut/peanut oil

90g/3oz (¾ cup) roughly chopped
carrots

100g/3½ oz (¾ cup) roughly
chopped onions

150ml/5fl oz (½ cup + 2 Tbl) dry
white wine

60g/2oz (4 Tbl) tomato
purée/paste

1 bouquet garni

1 bunch fresh mint – roughly
chopped

4 sachets tea (Earl Grey or any
personal favourite)

150g/5oz (10 Tbl) butter – in
pieces

salt and freshly ground black
pepper to taste

To garnish
sprigs of fresh mint

1 In a large, heavy-bottomed pan, brown the lamb bones in the oil.

2 Add the carrots and onions and cook until golden brown.

3 Pour in the wine and scrape the bottom of the pan to incorporate the caramelized cooking bits.

4 Stir in the tomato purée, add the bouquet garni, cover with water and simmer for 1 hour.

5 Add the fresh mint and the tea sachets and simmer for 30 minutes.

6 Pass the sauce through a sieve into a clean saucepan. Whisking constantly, gradually add the butter to finish the sauce.

7 Meanwhile, preheat the oven to 240°C/475°F/Gas Mark 9.

8 Cut the lamb fillets into medallions approximately 2.5cm/1in thick. Season with salt and freshly ground pepper and arrange on a rack in the roasting tin.

9 Roast, turning once, until golden but still slightly pink: approximately 10 minutes. The fillets should not be cooked through; they will continue to cook after being removed from the oven and should be "pink" when served.

10 Thinly cover the bottom of 4 heated serving plates with the sauce and arrange the medallions on top. Garnish with fresh mint sprigs and serve at once.

Serves 4

Equipment
roasting tin/pan with rack

NOTES

Steamed cauliflower goes
particularly well with this dish.

VEAL AND SALMON FILLETS IN SOURED CREAM PASTRY WITH TARRAGON SAUCE

CONTRIBUTED BY CHEF ROBERT SPETH
CHESERY GSTAAD, GSTAAD, SWITZERLAND

INGREDIENTS

For the soured cream pastry
250g/8¾ oz (2 ¼ cups) plain/all
   purpose flour
¼ tsp salt
75g/2½ oz (5 Tbl) unsalted butter
120g/4oz (½ cup) soured cream –
   room temperature
1 Tbl dry sherry or white wine
   vinegar

For the fish stuffing
75g/2½ oz salmon
70ml/2½fl oz (5 Tbl) double/heavy
   cream – cold
freshly grated nutmeg
salt and freshly ground white
   pepper

For the meat stuffing
75g/2½ oz veal or chicken
70ml/2½fl oz (5 Tbl) double/heavy
   cream – cold
freshly grated nutmeg
salt and freshly ground white
   pepper

The vegetables
175g/6oz (1½ cups) assorted
   "turned" vegetables: carrots,
   courgette/zucchini, kohlrabi
small broccoli florets – trimmed to
   the same size

Continued opposite

Prepare the pastry:
1 First be sure all the ingredients are at room temperature.
2 Sift the flour and salt into a large bowl. With fingers, rub in the butter.
3 Add the soured cream and vinegar and mix by hand to a smooth consistency.
4 Wrap in clingfilm and refrigerate for at least 6 hours.

Prepare the fish stuffing:
1 Cut the fish into small cubes. Sprinkle heavily with salt and pepper, cover and refrigerate for at least 1 hour.
2 Place the mixture and the cold cream into a food processor or blender and purée until smooth.
3 Force through a sieve. Add freshly grated nutmeg, taste and adjust seasoning, then cover and set aside.

Prepare the meat stuffing:
1 Repeat the fish stuffing method using the veal or chicken instead of the fish.

Prepare the vegetables:
1 Steam the vegetables briefly then quickly rinse in cold water (to keep their colour).
2 Drain, cover with clingfilm and reserve.

Serves 6 to 8

Equipment
food processor or blender
baking sheet/tray – greased
clingfilm/plastic wrap
fine sieve/chinois

NOTES

"Turning" vegetables simply means cutting them attractively into regularly sized pieces so they cook evenly. Using a very sharp knife, cut the vegetables into uniformly sized logs. Turning the logs in one hand, trim them into uniform "olive" shapes by paring the sides with even strokes (traditionally each shape has 7 even sides).

Cook the wild rice:

1 Thoroughly wash the wild rice in cold running water and then drain well.

2 Boil the water in a heavy-bottomed pan. Add the rice, cover tightly, and cook over low heat until the water is absorbed: approximately 45 minutes. It is cooked when the grains are swollen and cracked down the sides. Avoid overcooking.

Prepare the fillets:

1 Remove the pastry from the refrigerator – set aside.

2 In a frying pan, heat the oil until quite hot. Carefully brown the veal fillet for 2 to 3 minutes on each side.

3 Season the veal and leave to cool on a rack.

4 In a large pot of boiling salted water briefly blanch the spinach or lettuce leaves, drain and leave to cool.

5 On two clean tea towels, arrange the spinach/lettuce leaves in slightly overlapping fashion to form 2 rectangles, each one large enough to wrap one of the fillets.

6 Thinly spread half the salmon stuffing on one rectangle, and half the meat stuffing on the other.

7 Place the salmon fillet on the rectangle spread with salmon and wrap the fish in the spinach.

8 When the veal is cool, wrap it up in the remaining rectangle.

9 Preheat the oven to its highest setting.

10 Roll out the room-temperature pastry into a rectangle large enough to enclose both fillets, one on top of the other.

11 Spread the remaining stuffing along the long side of one fillet. Using this stuffing, stick the two fillets together.

12 Enclose the fillets in a pastry parcel. Brush with a mixture of beaten egg yolk and salt and leave to rest for 10 minutes.

13 Brush again with the egg mixture, place on a greased baking tray and cook for 5 minutes. Lower the heat to 220°C/425°F/ Gas Mark 8 and cook for a further 5 to 7 minutes.

14 Remove from the hot oven and allow to rest for 5 to 7 minutes in a warm place.

INGREDIENTS

285g/10oz (1½ cups) wild rice
700ml/1¼ pints (3 cups) water

For the veal and salmon fillets
2 Tbl grapeseed or
    groundnut/peanut oil
350g/12oz veal fillet – bone
    removed
300–350g/10–12oz salmon fillet
    (the same length and width as
    the veal)
100g/3½ oz leaf spinach or
    Cos/Romaine lettuce
1 egg yolk
salt

Continued overleaf

INGREDIENTS

For the tarragon sauce
60ml/2fl oz (¼ cup) dry white
    wine
30ml/1fl oz (2 Tbl) Noilly Prat
    (dry vermouth)
265ml/9fl oz (1 cup + 2 Tbl)
    unsalted stock (fish, vegetable or
    veal)
150ml/5fl oz (½ cup + 2 Tbl)
    double/heavy cream
10g/¼ oz (½ Tbl) unsalted butter –
    in cubes
a few drops tarragon vinegar
fresh tarragon to taste – finely
    chopped
1 tsp fresh lemon juice
½ Tbl double/heavy cream –
    whipped cream
cayenne pepper
salt and freshly ground white
    pepper to taste

For the vegetables
15g/½ oz (1 Tbl) unsalted butter
3 Tbl veal stock or water
fresh chervil to taste – chopped
fresh parsley to taste – chopped
fresh chives to taste – snipped

Prepare the sauce:
1 In a saucepan, reduce the wine and Noilly Prat by half.
2 Add the stock and any accumulated meat juices and reduce to
a fifth of its volume.
3 Pour in the cream and cook for 30 seconds.
4 Gradually whisk in the butter.
5 Stir in the vinegar, fresh tarragon, lemon juice and whipped
cream.
6 Season to taste with cayenne pepper and salt and freshly
ground white pepper.

Reheat the vegetables:
1 In a pan, heat the butter and stock.
2 Add the herbs and the blanched vegetables and toss until
heated through.

To serve:
1 Reheat the wild rice if necessary by tossing it in a saucepan
with melted butter.
2 Slice the parcel of fillets and arrange on heated plates.
Surround the slices with the sauce, garnish with the vegetables
and wild rice and serve immediately.

NOTES

Wild rice is the seed of an aquatic
grass and not an uncultivated
variety of common rice, to which
it is only distantly related. Its
chewy texture, brownish colour
and earthy flavour varies greatly
depending upon the river or lake
in which it was cultivated and how
it was harvested and processed.
Recently a shorter-grain variety of
wild rice has been paddy
cultivated. While this product is
less characteristic it is also much
less expensive.

Venison Sausage with Lentil Salad

CONTRIBUTED BY CHEF TED FONDULAS
HEMINGWAY'S RESTAURANT, KILLINGTON, VERMONT, USA

1 A day ahead combine all the ingredients for the venison stuffing in a large bowl. Cover and allow to marinate in the refrigerator overnight.

2 The following day, prepare the rabbit mixture: heat the butter in a pan and sweat the rabbit, mushrooms, shallots and leeks – drain and cool.

3 Using the medium die of a meat grinder, twice grind the marinated venison ingredients.

4 Fold the cooled rabbit mixture into the ground venison mixture and season with salt and freshly ground black pepper to taste. Sauté a spoonful of sausage mixture to taste the seasoning if you prefer not to taste the uncooked mixture.

5 Tie one end of a casing and pipe in the sausage mixture (tying in links as you go along). Repeat with remaining mixture and casings.

6 Prepare a wood smoker and preheat the oven to 200°C/400°F/Gas Mark 6.

7 Smoke the sausages for 4 minutes.

8 Remove from the smoker and place in the oven for 8 minutes.

9 Remove from the oven and allow to cool.

INGREDIENTS

For the venison stuffing
900g/2lb venison trimmings
175g/6oz fat back/salt pork or
    streaky green bacon
1 Tbl Armagnac
2 Tbl Port
1 Tbl fresh thyme leaves
1 Tbl chopped fresh
    coriander/cilantro
½ tsp ground cinnamon
a pinch ground clove
a pinch ground nutmeg
½ tsp grated fresh ginger
a pinch cayenne
30g/1oz (2 Tbl) butter
60g/2oz (¼ cup) currants

For the rabbit stuffing
30g/1oz (2 Tbl) butter
120g/4oz (½ cup) rabbit meat –
    diced
175g/6oz (1½ cups) sliced button
    mushrooms
90g/3oz (½ cup) chopped shallots
120g/4oz (1 cup) chopped leeks

To finish
salt and freshly ground black
    pepper to taste
pork casings cut into 60cm/2ft
    lengths

Continued opposite

Serves 4

Equipment
wood smoker (with maple or
    cherry wood, ideally)
meat grinder and sausage stuffer
kitchen string

NOTES

Serves 8 as a starter.

Pork casings can be ordered from quality butcher shops. Soak them in a bowl of cold water for 1 hour before using, then rinse thoroughly under cold running water (attach one opening to the tap and allow the water to flow through the casing). Tie one end of the casing tightly with kitchen string then slip the open end over the sausage nozzle/funnel and slide the casing up on to the nozzle until the closed end is at the nozzle's mouth.

Make the curried lemon vinaigrette:
1 Blend together the lemon juice, mint and oil.
2 Whisk in the curry paste and season to taste.
3 Pour into a salad bowl.

Make the balsamic vinaigrette:
1 Whisk all the ingredients together.
2 Add to the salad bowl.

Serve the dish:
1 Reheat the sausages in a preheated oven for 2 minutes.
2 Add the lentil salad ingredients to the dressings in the bowl and toss well.
3 Arrange the sausages on plates garnished with salad greens and serve immediately.

INGREDIENTS

For the curried lemon vinaigrette
dash of fresh lemon juice
½ tsp chopped fresh mint
3 Tbl olive oil
¼ tsp curry paste
salt and freshly ground black
    pepper to taste

For the balsamic vinaigrette
3 Tbl olive oil
1 Tbl balsamic vinegar
a few drops boiling water
salt and freshly ground black
    pepper to taste

For the lentil salad
340g/12oz (2 cups) cooked
    French green lentils
120g/4oz (½ cup) finely diced
    carrot
90g/3oz (½ cup) finely diced
    courgette/zucchini

Serve with
field greens/mixed salad leaves

To make extra vinaigrette for use in other recipes, follow the quantities given below. Keep in tightly sealed jars and use within 24 hours. For the curried lemon vinaigrette: 1½ Tbl fresh lemon juice, 2 Tbl chopped fresh mint, 470ml/16fl oz (2 cups) olive oil, 1 Tbl curry paste and salt and freshly ground black pepper to taste. For the balsamic vinaigrette: 470ml/16fl oz (2 cups) olive oil, 120ml/4fl oz (½ cup) balsamic vinegar, 1 Tbl boiling water and salt and freshly ground black pepper to taste.

SADDLE OF RABBIT WITH BASIL

CONTRIBUTED BY CHEF FRÉDY GIRARDET
GIRARDET, LAUSANNE, SWITZERLAND

INGREDIENTS

1 saddle of rabbit (from a
   2.5kg/5lb rabbit)
2 Tbl chopped fresh basil
1 Tbl olive oil
6 cloves garlic – unpeeled
4 shallots – peeled and quartered
100ml/3½fl oz (7 Tbl) dry white
   wine or chicken stock
1 Tbl jus or fond de veau/reduced
   veal stock
50g/1¾oz (3 1/2 Tbl) butter – in
   cubes
salt and freshly ground black
   pepper to taste

Serve with
a seasonal vegetable purée and
   paillasson potatoes

1 Preheat the oven to 180°C/350°F/Gas Mark 4.

2 Trim the rabbit and make cuts the length of the saddle along either side of the backbone, slicing through to the bone.

3 Insert half the chopped basil into these two cuts and season with salt and freshly ground black pepper.

4 In an ovenproof pan, heat the oil and add the garlic and shallots.

5 Place the saddle in the pan and turn it until the outside just turns white on all sides – do not allow it to colour at all. Then place the pan in the oven for 12 minutes, basting frequently.

6 Remove the rabbit, place on a serving dish and keep warm.

7 Return the cooking pan to the burner, add the wine or stock and the fond de veau and bring to a simmer, stirring to incorporate the caramelized cooking juices. Simmer until the garlic and shallots are cooked through, then pour the sauce mixture into a blender, food processor or mill, and purée.

8 Pour the purée into a small saucepan over medium heat and reduce slightly.

9 Add the remaining basil and whisk in the butter. Taste and season with salt and pepper.

10 Cut the rabbit along its length into serving pieces. Serve immediately on heated plates with the sauce spooned over the meat.

Serves 2 to 3

Equipment
blender, food processor or
   mouli mill
ovenproof pan

NOTES

Rable de Lapin au Basilic (French)

To prepare paillasson ("doormat") potatoes, first cut peeled uncooked potatoes into very fine julienne strips. In a non-stick frying pan, heat a little oil until very hot then evenly scatter a thin layer of potato over the oil. Pat it down to form a "mat", season with salt and pepper and cook until the bottom is crisp and browned and the top cooked through. Transfer to a hot plate (browned side up) and repeat with the remaining potatoes.

FRICASSEE OF YOUNG RABBIT WITH CHANTERELLES AND GARDEN PEAS

CONTRIBUTED BY CHEF CHRISTOPHE CHASTELLAIN
RESTAURANT LA BAGATELLE, HOTEL LE GRAND CHALET, GSTAAD, SWITZERLAND

INGREDIENTS

4 fillets cut from 2 cleaned and
  boned rabbit saddles
100g/3½oz (1 cup) best
  chanterelles
80g/2¾oz (¾ cup) shelled garden
  peas
40g/1½oz (3 Tbl) unsalted butter
1½ Tbl finely diced shallots
100ml/3½fl oz (scant ½ cup) white
  wine (Mont-sur-Rolle or a light
  Chablis)
200ml/7fl oz (a generous ¾ cup)
  crème fraîche
salt and freshly ground black
  pepper to taste

1 Cut the rabbit fillets into 20g/¾oz cubes.

2 Very briefly rinse the chanterelles under cold running water and allow to drain.

3 Briefly blanch the peas (in lightly salted boiling water) then immediately place them in iced water to preserve their fresh colour — reserve.

4 In a large frying pan, heat 20g/¾oz (1½ Tbl) of the butter until it bubbles slightly.

5 Add the rabbit pieces and half the shallots and season with salt and freshly ground black pepper.

6 Over high heat, lightly brown the meat, stirring constantly for 1 minute (do not let it get too brown).

7 Remove from the heat and place the meat in a sieve to drain away any excess butter.

8 Return the hot pan to the heat and add the remaining 20g/¾oz (1½ Tbl) butter, the chanterelles and the remaining shallots. Lightly brown the mushrooms over gentle heat and season with salt.

9 Pour in the wine, stir to deglaze the pan, gently incorporate the caramelized cooking residue and reduce by half.

10 Add the crème fraîche and allow the sauce to reduce until it coats the back of a metal spoon.

11 Return the rabbit to the pan, add the peas and bring slowly to the boil. Remove from the heat and check seasoning.

12 Serve in heated soup plates with a small amount of sauce.

Serves 4

NOTES

Fricassée de Lapereau aux Chanterelles et Pois Gourmands (French)

Since the flavour of this delicate dish depends upon the freshness of the ingredients, use only the freshest young rabbit and the best fresh chanterelles and peas.

Chanterelles (Cantharellus cibarius) are highly prized, golden-coloured, funnel-shaped wild mushrooms. They must be cooked gently to avoid toughening and should be only lightly seasoned to enhance their sophisticated flavour.

Crème fraîche is a matured, thickened cream, with a sharp but not sour flavour. It is widely available in supermarkets.

RABBIT CHASSEUR

CONTRIBUTED BY NORMA MAJOR, LONDON

1 In a large frying pan, heat the oil with half of the butter.

2 Pat the rabbit pieces dry with paper towelling, lie them in the pan and scatter the onion over them. Cook over a low to moderate heat for 15 to 20 minutes.

3 Sprinkle the flour over the rabbit in the pan, stir in the tomato purée, wine and stock, and cover. Simmer gently for 30 minutes, until the rabbit is tender.

4 Meanwhile, in another frying pan, heat the remaining butter and lightly sauté the mushroom pieces. Ten minutes before the rabbit is fully cooked, add the sautéed mushrooms.

5 Transfer the rabbit and mushrooms to a heated serving dish and keep warm.

6 Over high heat, reduce the sauce to a syrupy consistency. Taste and season with salt and pepper if necessary.

7 Spoon the sauce over the rabbit, garnish with croûtons and parsley and serve immediately on heated plates.

Serves 4

Equipment
frying pan or casserole with lid

INGREDIENTS

2 Tbl non-scented oil

30g/1oz (2 Tbl) unsalted butter

1 young rabbit – skinned, jointed and well soaked

1 Tbl finely chopped onion

1 Tbl plain/all purpose flour

1 tsp tomato purée

90ml/3oz (6 Tbl) dry white wine

600ml/20fl oz (2½ cups) chicken or veal stock

225g/8oz (2 cups) button mushrooms – cleaned, trimmed and quartered

salt and freshly ground black pepper to taste

To garnish
croûtons
a little chopped fresh parsley

Serve with
mashed potatoes and colourful seasonal vegetables

NOTES

Button mushrooms (Agaricus bisporus) are immature cultivated mushrooms, harvested just as they break the surface. The caps are still tightly closed, the stems very short and the flesh white. Widely available and moderately priced, they have a pleasant texture and delicate flavour. They are frequently eaten raw, either in salads or marinated, or added to simmered dishes because they absorb and complement other flavours readily. To clean, brush gently then wipe with kitchen paper because exposure to water deteriorates their subtle flavour.

To make croûtons, heat non-scented oil (at least 1cm/½in deep) in a frying pan until very hot, add bread cubes (stale bread fries better than fresh, as it absorbs less oil), turn once, remove and drain on paper towelling. Remember that the croûtons will continue to cook even after you remove them from the pan so be careful to take them out when they are just beginning to turn golden brown.

BRAISED RABBIT WITH FARMHOUSE VEGETABLES

CONTRIBUTED BY CHEF SHAUN THOMSON
WHITE'S, LONDON

1 Preheat the oven to 220°C/425°F/Gas Mark 7.

2 In a large frying pan, heat the oil.

3 Fry the pieces of rabbit and the liver and kidneys until sealed — remove and arrange in a casserole.

4 Add the vegetables, mushrooms and garlic to the frying pan, sauté until they start to soften then remove and add to the casserole.

5 Add the herbs, tomato purée, soaked prunes and cider to the casserole, cover and place in the oven for 30 minutes.

6 Arrange the rabbit and vegetables artfully on a heated serving plate (slicing the liver and kidneys) and serve immediately.

INGREDIENTS

1 Tbl olive oil

1 small farmed rabbit – cleaned and jointed (liver and kidneys reserved)

225g/8oz (2 cups) carrots – in 1cm/½in cubes

120g/4oz (1 cup) swede/rutabaga – in 1cm/½in cubes

120g/4oz celeriac (1 cups) – in 1cm/½in cubes

8 button/pearl onions – peeled

8 button mushrooms – in 1cm/½in pieces

2 cloves garlic – chopped

2 or 3 sprigs fresh thyme

2 or 3 sprigs fresh marjoram

2 Tbl tomato purée/paste

4 prunes – soaked in cider to cover for 30 minutes

600ml/20fl oz (2½ cups) dry cider

Serves 2

Equipment
casserole with lid

NOTES

This recipe is for a small, farmed rabbit. If using a large one, double the quantities; and if using a wild rabbit, double the cooking time. Ask the butcher to clean the rabbit, retaining the liver and kidneys, and prepare it so that you are left with the front and back legs and the saddle fillets for this dish. Reserve the bones and trimmings for making game stock.

To peel small onions, immerse them briefly in boiling water then quickly place in cold water – the skin will then come off easily.

SUKIYAKI

....

CONTRIBUTED BY THE HOTEL OKURA, TOKYO, JAPAN

INGREDIENTS

900g/2lb well-marbled sirloin beef
 – very thinly sliced
400g/14oz shirataki noodles,
 drained
200g/7oz tinned bamboo shoots,
 drained
400g/14oz yaki-dofu, drained
340g/12oz (3 cups) slender young
 leeks (white and tender green
 parts) – cut on the diagonal
 into 5cm/2in segments
450g/1lb (3 cups) onions – sliced
 in thin segments
6 fresh shiitake mushrooms –
 stems removed and tops
 notched
300g/10½oz enoki mushrooms –
 drained, spongy root removed
200g/7oz fresh shungiku (edible
 chrysanthemum leaves) or
 tender young spinach leaves
 with tough stems removed

For the braising sauce
150ml/5fl oz (⅔ cup) light soy
 sauce (preferably Japanese)
180ml/6fl oz (¾ cup) mirin
2 level tsp granulated sugar
90ml/3fl oz (6 Tbl) beef stock

For the dipping sauce
6 fresh eggs

Continued opposite

120

Prepare the ingredients:
1 Ensure the beef is in paper-thin slices. See Notes, below.
2 Cut the shirataki noodles into 9cm/3in lengths, place in a strainer and pour boiling water over. Drain and cool.
3 Slice the bamboo shoots into vertical wedges that look like combs, removing any white calcified material from between the "teeth" of the combs.
4 Cut the cake of grilled bean curd – yaki-dofu – in half lengthways, then across twice to yield 6 cubes.
5 On a large serving platter, arrange the beef, noodles, bamboo shoots, bean curd, leeks, onions, shiitake mushrooms, enoki mushrooms and leaves.
6 In a small saucepan, combine the braising sauce ingredients and bring to a boil, stirring. Transfer to a serving jug.
7 Arrange the table: each person has a pair of chopsticks (or fondue fork) and two bowls, one empty and one containing a raw egg. The egg can be gently beaten with the chopsticks and used as a dipping sauce. Most Tokyo residents enjoy this egg sauce, but it is not essential to the dish.

Serves 6

Equipment
table-top burner – optional
shallow cast-iron pan or electric
 frying pan

NOTES

The beef should be in paper-thin slices. Ask your butcher to do this, or place the meat in the freezer briefly to stiffen it and make slicing easier.

Shirataki (white waterfall) noodles are sold packed in liquid (often with a peculiar odour) in most oriental groceries. Drain and lightly blanch before use.

Yaki-dofu is a compressed and grilled block of tofu. Regular "firm-style" tofu may be substituted.

Enoki mushrooms (Flammulina velutipes) are very pale mushrooms with long thin stems and tightly closed tiny caps. They grow in clumps and their spongy bottoms must be removed or trimmed before serving. Originally from Japan, they are now cultivated and widely available in western markets.

Mirin is a sweetened rice wine used in Japanese kitchens. It is widely available.

Prepare the dish:

1 If using a table-top burner or electric frying pan, place it in the centre of the table with the platter of ingredients, the jug of braising sauce and the suet or oil. (The cooking can, of course, be done on the kitchen stove if preferred.)

2 Heat the frying pan and melt the suet or heat a few drops of vegetable oil (just enough to keep the first ingredients from sticking).

3 Start the cooking with the leeks and onions, pushing them aside as they brown slightly.

4 Add about one-quarter of the meat, pushing it aside as it changes colour.

5 Pour in about one-third of the braising stock.

6 Add some of the mushrooms, leaves and bamboo shoots and cook briefly.

7 Each person can now begin helping themselves to the food as it cooks by selecting a few bits and placing them in their empty bowl, then dipping the vegetables and meat into the egg sauce if desired – the egg "cooks" on contact with the hot food.

8 Replenish the pan with fresh ingredients and adjust the amount of braising liquid as the food cooks.

9 Cook the noodles and bean curd during the second half of the meal when a fair amount of gravy has accumulated for these porous ingredients to soak up.

Although one-pot table-top cooking is a traditional Japanese cooking style, beef was introduced into Japan only by western diplomats in the 1860s. The name of this dish (which literally means "cooked on a ploughshare") reflects initial reluctance to contaminate cooking utensils by contact with beef. Sukiyaki is now a favourite celebratory dish, not only delicious but also guaranteed to create a festive mood for young or old. There is intense, good-natured culinary rivalry between Tokyo and Osaka. This version is Tokyo-style; Osaka-style does not simmer the braising sauce beforehand but mixes it directly in the cooking pan.

Enoki may be eaten raw or simmered briefly: they need only seconds to cook and if overdone become stringy and tasteless.

INGREDIENTS

To cook the meal
15g/1/2 oz (1 Tbl) beef suet or a
few drops of vegetable oil

To follow the meal
Japanese rice and a colourful
selection of Japanese pickles
(enormous varieties of which
are available in oriental markets)

SICHUAN DOUBLE-COOKED PORK

CONTRIBUTED BY CHEF KENNETH H. C. LO
KEN LO'S MEMORIES OF CHINA RESTAURANT, LONDON

INGREDIENTS

1kg/2lb 3oz belly of pork – in one
  piece
1 tsp salt
4 Tbl vegetable oil
340g/12oz (3 cups) young tender
  leeks – thoroughly washed and
  cut into 3cm/1¼in segments
  (white and tender green parts)
4 Tbl good chicken stock
additional salt to taste

For the sauce
3 cloves garlic – finely chopped
4 slices fresh ginger – finely
  chopped
3 spring onions/scallions – finely
  chopped
2 Tbl dark soy sauce
2 Tbl tomato sauce
2 Tbl hoisin sauce
2 Tbl light soy sauce
2 Tbl good chicken stock
2 tsp oriental chilli sauce or
  Tabasco Sauce

Serve with
copious amounts of boiled or
  steamed white rice

1 Bring a large pan of water to the boil, add the pork and salt and simmer gently for 45 minutes.

2 In a small bowl, mix all the sauce ingredients together – set aside.

3 Remove the pan with the simmering pork from the heat and add 1 litre/34fl oz (4¼ cups) cold water. Leave for 10 minutes, then remove and drain the pork.

4 Remove excess fat and slice the pork across the grain into thin slices approximately 5cm/2in square.

5 Heat the oil in a wok or large frying pan. When hot, add the leeks, stir-fry for 2 minutes and remove – set them aside.

6 Add the pork to the same pan, pour the sauce over it and stir-fry over high heat for 2 minutes, coating all the slices thoroughly with the sauce.

7 Add the leeks to one side of the pork, sprinkle with the stock and salt to taste.

8 Bring to the boil (1 minute), then serve immediately on a heated serving dish, placing pork slices in the centre and surrounding them with the leeks.

Serves 4 to 6

Equipment
wok or large frying pan

NOTES

Dark soy sauce is aged longer and is therefore slightly thicker and stronger than light soy sauce. It is available in oriental markets where it is labelled "Soy Superior Sauce". Check the label carefully because light soy is labelled "Superior Soy".

Hoisin sauce ("fresh sea sauce") is a thick soy- and vinegar-based brownish-red sauce with a sweet and slightly spicy flavour. Often served with Peking duck, it is widely available and frequently labelled Chinese barbecue sauce. Hoisin keeps almost indefinitely if tightly sealed and refrigerated.

TIFFIN PORK CHOPS

CONTRIBUTED BY CHEF TERRY TAN, LONDON

INGREDIENTS

4 loin pork chops – trimmed and
   boned
1 egg – lightly beaten
10 Jacob's Cream Crackers –
   finely crushed
oil for deep-frying

For the sauce
2 Tbl groundnut/peanut oil
½ large onion – finely sliced
1 tsp cornflour/cornstarch
6 Tbl water
2 Tbl HP Sauce (or A-1 Sauce)
1 Tbl tomato ketchup
1 Tbl dark soy sauce
½ tsp freshly ground black pepper

Serve with
white rice, or any two seasonal
   vegetables such as glazed
   carrots, peas, mashed potatoes
   or swedes with a bit of butter,
   or Indian naan bread

1 With a mallet, lightly beat the pork chops to tenderize them (each should be about 1cm/⅓in thick).
2 Prepare 2 shallow bowls, one with the lightly beaten egg, the other with the cracker crumbs.
3 First dredge each chop in egg then roll in crumbs – set aside for the coating to "take" (approximately 3 minutes).
4 Heat the oil and deep-fry the chops, two at a time, until crisp and golden brown – keep warm.

Prepare the sauce and serve:
1 While the chops are frying, in a separate frying pan heat the oil and fry the onion until soft but not brown.
2 In a bowl, dissolve the cornflour in the water. Blend the remaining sauce ingredients into this mixture.
3 Add the mixture to the onions, bring to a slow boil and immediately remove from the heat.
4 Serve the chops, either with the sauce poured over them or passed separately on the side.

Serves 4

NOTES

While sowing the seeds of fortunes for themselves, British planters also created enclaves of Britannia in Asia. Imported products being at a premium, creative cooks produced famous "western-style sauces" from local fruits and spices. These sauces, which include various ketchups, Worcestershire and HP sauces, have become enduring favourites at British tables worldwide. The colonial legacy in Singaporean cuisine features "Tiffin" (lunch box) specialities, such as this recipe, which combined British fare with tasty local adaptations.

Jacob's Cream Crackers are a popular UK brand of plain savoury biscuits frequently served with cheese. American soda crackers or other mild unsalted ones are the closest substitute in the US.

Ketchup (from the Malay "ketjap") is the generic term for a spicy sweet and sour sauce that includes salt, sugar, vinegar and a variety of spices. In Asia, seafood-based ketchups are popular but in the west they are usually made from fruits, vegetables or nuts, with tomato and mushroom varieties being particularly popular.

FILLET STEAK WITH CELERIAC AND MOREL MUSHROOMS

CONTRIBUTED BY CHEF SHAUN HILL
GIDLEIGH PARK, CHAGFORD, DEVON, ENGLAND

Serves 4

Equipment
blender – optional
copper or iron skillet/frying pan

1 Soak the dried morels in cold water (1 to 2 hours) then slice them lengthways, remove the stalks and wash thoroughly – reserve.

2 Peel the celeriac, split it in half and cut one half into cubes, the other into thin strips. Set the strips aside in water to which lemon juice has been added.

3 Boil the celeriac cubes in salted water until tender. Drain and mash or process in a blender, season with salt and freshly ground white pepper and and add the cream – keep in a warm place.

4 Preheat a copper or iron pan, brush the steaks with olive oil and pan-fry to the desired doneness (about 4 minutes each side for medium rare). Remove from the pan and keep warm.

5 Add the stock to the pan, scraping the bottom to incorporate any browned bits, then add the morels and boil until the liquid thickens (about 2 minutes).

6 Meanwhile, in another frying pan, heat the butter and fry the celeriac strips until golden brown. Drain on kitchen paper and keep warm.

7 Put a good spoonful of celeriac purée on each heated dinner plate, cover with a fillet steak, top with celeriac strips, spoon mushroom sauce around and serve immediately.

INGREDIENTS

30g/1oz dried morel mushrooms
1.4kg/3lb celeriac
splash of lemon juice
120ml/4fl oz (½ cup)
   double/heavy cream
4 × 175g/6oz beef fillet steaks
1 tsp olive oil
300ml/10fl oz (1¼ cup) reduced
   veal stock
30g/1oz (2 Tbl) unsalted butter
salt and freshly ground white
   pepper

NOTES

Morel mushrooms, highly prized and considered the only flavour rival to truffles, have conical caps with a honeycombed, spongy appearance. Because of their irregular indentations, they need careful cleaning before use.

Celeriac/celery root or knob is a light-coloured, rough-surfaced root vegetable with a nutty, sweet flavour. It is related to but is not the root of common celery. It can be eaten raw (cut into julienne strips and dressed with mayonnaise). Celeriac flesh discolours quickly on contact with air – hold cut pieces in acidulated water (water with fresh lemon juice in it) prior to cooking.

VEGETABLES
AND
PASTA

SPICY SWEET POTATO AND CHESTNUT GRATIN

CONTRIBUTED BY CHEF CHARLES WILEY
THE BOULDERS, CAREFREE, ARIZONA, USA

INGREDIENTS

235ml/8fl oz (1 cup) double/heavy
cream
4 Tbl pure maple syrup
3 cloves garlic – roasted
2 ancho chillies – stems and seeds
removed and flesh torn into
1cm/½in pieces
2 or 3 (depending on size) sweet
potatoes – peeled and very
thinly sliced
3 leeks (white parts only) – sliced
90g/3oz (½ cup) coarsely chopped
roasted chestnuts
120g/4oz (1 cup) shredded aged
Monterey Jack cheese
kosher salt and freshly ground
black pepper to taste

To garnish
snipped fresh chives

Serve with
roast rack of lamb with a pecan
cornbread crust

1 In a small saucepan, heat the cream.

2 Add the maple syrup, roasted garlic and chilli pieces and steep for 30 minutes.

3 Preheat the oven to 180°C/350°C/Gas Mark 4.

4 Purée the cream mixture in a food processor or blender until smooth.

5 Arrange about a third of the potatoes in a layer in the buttered casserole, overlapping the slices slightly. Season with salt and freshly ground black pepper, pour a third of the cream mixture over and top with a third of the leeks, chestnuts and shredded cheese.

6 Repeat step 5 two more times with the remaining ingredients.

7 Cover and bake for 40 minutes.

8 Uncover the gratin and bake for another 20 minutes until brown and bubbly.

9 Allow to rest for 20 minutes then cut and serve, garnished with fresh chives.

Serves 6 to 8

Equipment
22 x 30cm/9 x 12in ovenproof
casserole with lid – lightly
buttered
food processor or blender

NOTES

To roast individual garlic cloves, first peel the cloves and place on a small sheet of foil. Coat them with olive oil and sprinkle with a little water and fold the foil into a closed parcel. Place in a 180°C/350°F/Gas Mark 4 oven for 30 minutes. Open the packet and continue to roast uncovered for 10 minutes until golden brown.

Ancho chillies (dried poblano chillies) are the most commonly used dried chillies in Mexican and southwestern US cooking. Available in speciality stores, they are usually about 10cm/4in long and 7.5cm/3in wide, with leathery mahogany-coloured flesh. Anchos have a complex spicy yet mildly fruity flavour with aromatic coffee and raisin overtones.

Asiago or Parmigiano-reggiano may be substituted for the Monterey Jack cheese.

VEGETABLE CURRY

CONTRIBUTED BY CHEF THAI LA ROCHE
THE HUNGRY MONK, JEVINGTON, SUSSEX, ENGLAND

1 Place the carrots, potatoes and parsnip in a pan with the boiling water and half cook. Drain and reserve the vegetables and 600ml/1 pint (2½ cups) of the stock.

2 In a large heavy casserole, heat the oil and add the onions, garlic, courgettes, celery, green pepper, tomatoes and mushrooms. Cook over low heat for a few minutes.

3 Stir in the curry powder and tomato paste.

4 Add the reserved carrots, potatoes and parsnip and stir well.

5 Add the reserved vegetable stock and bring sharply to the boil over high heat, then reduce the heat, partially cover and simmer to reduce the curry to a good consistency (about 25 minutes), stirring occasionally.

6 Add the apricots, kidney beans, chutney and pickles and warm them through. Meanwhile prepare the rice (see note below for ingredients and method).

7 Season the curry to taste and serve on heated plates surrounded by a ring of hot rice. Sprinkle with fresh coriander leaves and hand around other garnishes of your choice.

Serves 8 to 10

Equipment
large heavy flameproof casserole
  with lid

INGREDIENTS

2 large carrots, 2 large potatoes
  and 1 parsnip – peeled or
  scraped, and roughly chopped
945ml/32fl oz (4 cups) boiling
  salted water
10 Tbl sunflower or vegetable oil
2 medium onions – roughly
  chopped
2 cloves garlic – finely chopped
1 courgette/zucchini – roughly
  chopped
1 stick celery – roughly chopped
1 green bell pepper – cored,
  seeded and roughly chopped
6 tomatoes – peeled, seeded and
  roughly chopped
60g/2oz (½ cup) mushrooms –
  roughly chopped
2–6 Tbl medium curry powder –
  to taste
4 Tbl tinned tomato paste
115g/4oz (1 cup) tinned apricots
  – roughly chopped
225g/8oz (1 cup) tinned red
  kidney beans
2 Tbl chopped mango chutney
1 Tbl chopped Indian lime pickles
salt and freshly ground black
  pepper to taste

To garnish
chopped fresh coriander/cilantro

NOTES

For 8 to 10 people you need 500g/1lb 2oz (2½ cups) basmati or long-grain rice. If using basmati rice, rinse it under cold water. In a heavy-bottomed pan, bring 3 litres/5 pints (12½ cups) water to the boil and add 2 tsp salt. Stir in the rice, reduce the heat to medium and cook, uncovered, for 15–20 minutes. Drain, rinse in cool water and drain again. Warm the rice by placing it in a colander over simmering water, tossing frequently.

Additional garnishes that can be passed separately are chopped banana (coated in lemon juice to prevent discoloration), grated coconut and mango chutney. Poppadoms also make a good accompaniment.

SPRING VEGETABLE RISOTTO WITH PARMESAN

CONTRIBUTED BY SALLY CLARKE
CLARKE'S, LONDON

INGREDIENTS

450g/1lb pencil thin fresh
  asparagus spears – washed and
  trimmed
450g/1lb broad beans – podded
225g/8oz (1 cup) butter
2 medium onions – finely diced
285g/10oz (1½ cups) arborio rice
2 rounded tsp freshly chopped
  thyme leaves
210ml/7fl oz (¾ cup + 2 Tbl)
  good white wine
900ml/30fl oz (3¾ cups) warm
  water – or more if necessary
450g/1lb fresh peas – podded
good olive oil
salt and freshly ground black
  pepper to taste

To garnish
sprigs of fresh thyme
120g/4oz (1 cup) fine shavings of
  fresh Parmesan cheese
additional olive oil

Serve with
a crisp salad of garden leaves
  tossed with olive oil, fresh herbs
  and salt and pepper

1 Place 4 soup bowls/plates in the oven to warm.

2 Cut the asparagus stalks into 1cm/½in lengths and reserve the tips – set aside.

3 Blanch the broad beans for 15 seconds then peel – set aside.

4 In a heavy pan, melt half of the butter and add the onion. Stir until it just begins to soften but do not let it colour.

5 Add the rice and stir, thoroughly coating each rice grain with the butter.

6 Add the thyme, season with salt and pepper, then pour in the wine and stir gently until almost absorbed.

7 During the following 5–10 mins of slow cooking, add the warm water gradually – approximately 60ml/2fl oz (¼ cup) at a time – stirring until the liquid is almost absorbed before adding more water. You must stir constantly to achieve the right consistency and to prevent the rice from sticking to the pan bottom.

8 Keep tasting the rice to test for "doneness" (tender yet firm to the bite). When it is almost cooked through, add the asparagus stalks and half of the peas. Taste for seasoning; it should be quite flavourful.

9 When the rice is done, remove the pan from the heat, stir in the remaining butter and cover – set briefly aside.

10 Cook the asparagus tips, broad beans and the remaining peas in boiling salted water for a few seconds until just al dente. Drain and toss in olive oil to coat and season to taste.

11 Spoon the risotto into the hot serving bowls, top with the hot vegetables, garnish with thyme sprigs and serve as quickly as possible.

12 Scatter the shavings of Parmesan over each serving at the table and pass more olive oil and fresh black pepper if desired – eat at once.

Serves 4

NOTES

The quantity of liquid for risotto is approximate. It varies with the age of the rice, the way it was stored and even the annual rainfall in the area where it was grown. The trick is not to add too much liquid at one time, especially towards the end of the cooking time. The correct cooking heat is also important. It should be medium to high, but if the liquid evaporates too rapidly the rice will be soft outside and chalky inside. If too low, the rice will be sticky and gluey. Perfect risotto is al dente and creamy, neither dry nor runny.

Arborio (Italian short-grain rice) is a plump round-grained type of rice widely available in speciality food stores in both white and brown varieties. Its starchy texture makes it ideal for this dish. If it is not available, long-grain rice works almost as well, if carefully cooked.

MUSHROOM QUICHE

....

CONTRIBUTED BY BARBARA BUSH, HOUSTON, TEXAS, USA

INGREDIENTS

For the pastry case/pie crust
225g/8oz (1 cup) plain/all purpose
   flour
pinch of salt
150g/5oz (10 Tbl) of fat (butter,
   margarine, shortening, lard – or
   a combination of any 2)
3–4 Tbl cold water

Continued opposite

Prepare the pastry case:
1 Sift the flour and salt together in a mixing bowl.
2 With a knife, cut in the fat.
3 Rub with fingertips until the mixture resembles fine breadcrumbs.
4 Make a well in the centre and gradually add the water – you may not need all of it to make a firm dough.
5 Turn on to a floured board and knead lightly until smooth.
6 Wrap in greaseproof/waxed paper and allow to rest in the refrigerator for 20–30 minutes.
7 Preheat the oven to 200°C/400°F/Gas Mark 6.
8 On a floured board, roll the pastry out to the desired size.
9 Slide the pastry off the board on to the flan/pie tin. Press the pastry into position, easing it into the edges of the tin, and trim off excess.
10 Bake blind (see Notes) until golden brown and crisp (15 to 20 minutes). Set aside while you prepare the filling.

Serves 6

Equipment
22cm/9in deep flan/pie tin
greaseproof/waxed paper

NOTES

To bake blind, line the uncooked pastry shell with greaseproof paper or foil and fill it with pie weights, dried beans or rice – this keeps the pastry from bubbling up during cooking.

When you come to cook the filled quiche, place a baking tray/sheet on the oven rack while the oven is heating up and place the quiche on it to bake. This not only helps to cook the bottom of the pastry shell but also catches any spillage.

Prepare the filling and bake the quiche:

1 Position a rack in the lower third of the oven and preheat to 190°C/375°F/Gas Mark 5.

2 In a large frying pan over medium high heat, melt the butter.

3 Sauté the mushrooms, onion, garlic and shallots together until softened.

4 Stir in the herbs and seasonings, increase the heat and cook until the liquid has evaporated (about 2 minutes).

5 Remove from the heat and cool for 5 minutes.

6 In a medium bowl, combine the eggs with the cream or milk, beating well.

7 Stir the mushroom mixture into the egg mixture.

8 Pour the filling into the prepared pastry base.

9 Bake until the filling is puffed, set and starting to turn brown (approximately 35–45 minutes).

10 Serve warm or at room temperature, sprinkled with the fresh herbs.

When using dried herbs, rub them vigorously between the palms of your hand as you add them to release the flavourful oils. If using fresh herbs, double the recipe amounts to compensate for their more delicate flavour.

INGREDIENTS

For the quiche filling
45g/1½oz (3 Tbl) butter
560g/1lb 4oz fresh button mushrooms – sliced
3 spring onions/scallions – finely chopped
1 clove garlic – finely chopped
3 shallots – finely chopped
1¾ tsp dried oregano
1¾ tsp dried basil
¾ tsp dried marjoram
¼ tsp dried thyme
½ tsp dry mustard
1¼ tsp salt
¼ tsp freshly ground black pepper
4 eggs
180ml/6fl oz (¾ cup) single/light cream, milk or skimmed milk

To garnish
a sprinkling of chopped fresh herbs

Serve with
a green salad

OPRAH'S "CLASSIC" POTATOES

CONTRIBUTED BY OPRAH WINFREY, USA

1 Wash all the potatoes well, leaving the skin on. Cut into large even chunks.
2 Place in a large pan and cover with cold water.
3 Bring to the boil, lower the heat and simmer until the potatoes are very tender.
4 Drain off all the water and, while the potatoes are hot, add the butter and begin to mash with a potato masher.
5 Add the horseradish, cream, salt and pepper and mash until creamy but slightly lumpy. Serve at once.

INGREDIENTS

1.1kg/2½lb red potatoes
1.1kg/2½lb baking potatoes
  (preferably Idaho)
285g/10oz butter
300ml/10fl oz (1¼ cups) creamed
  puréed horseradish
700ml/24fl oz (3 cups)
  double/heavy cream
2½ Tbl kosher salt
1½ Tbl freshly ground black
  pepper

Serves 8 to 10

Equipment
potato masher

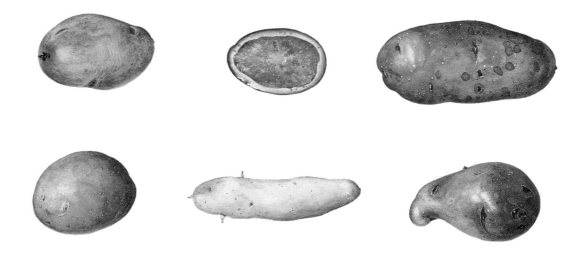

ONION CAKE

....

CONTRIBUTED BY GLENYS KINNOCK, PONTLLANFRAITH, WALES

1 Preheat the oven to 200°C/400°F/ Gas Mark 6.

2 Cut the potatoes into paper-thin slices using a food processor if available.

3 Wash the potato slices well in plenty of cold water (to remove starch) and dry thoroughly in a clean kitchen towel.

4 Arrange alternate layers of potatoes and onions in your baking dish, dotting each layer with small pieces of butter and seasoning as you go (don't worry if the potato comes a bit above the rim of the dish, it will cook down).

5 Cover the dish with foil and bake for 45 minutes. Remove foil and bake for an additional 15 minutes.

6 Turn out the Feiser Nionod (its Welsh name) on to a heated serving plate or serve it piping hot right out of the gratin dish.

Serves 8

Equipment
food processor – optional
large baking tin, gratin dish or
   shallow casserole – well
   buttered

INGREDIENTS

....

900g/2lb firm white potatoes –
   peeled
450g/1lb English/common onions
   – chopped
120g/4oz (8 Tbl) butter
salt and freshly ground black
   pepper to taste

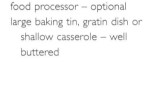

TOMATO SOUFFLÉ

CONTRIBUTED BY THE CARLTON CLUB, LONDON

INGREDIENTS

8 large, firm tomatoes
45g/1½oz (3 Tbl) butter – at room temperature
8 fresh basil leaves – chopped
3 eggs – separated
100g/3½oz (¾ cup) grated Gruyère cheese
35g/1¼oz (¼ cup) plain/all purpose flour
3 Tbl single/light cream
a pinch of medium paprika
salt and freshly ground black pepper to taste

To garnish
watercress sprigs

1 Preheat the oven to 180°C/350°F/Gas Mark 4.
2 Wash the tomatoes. Cut off the tops and reserve them.
3 Carefully scoop out the tomato flesh, leaving the shells intact. Discard the seeds and finely dice the flesh – reserve.
4 Season the insides of the tomato shells with salt and pepper and stand them upside down on kitchen paper to drain.
5 In a large bowl, beat the butter with the chopped basil until creamy.
6 Gradually fold the egg yolks, cheese, flour, cream and reserved tomato flesh into the butter mixture.
7 In a clean dry bowl, beat the egg whites until stiff and dry. Gently fold into the tomato mixture and season to taste.
8 Fill the reserved tomato shells with the cheese soufflé mixture and place in a shallow baking dish. Bake for 20 minutes or until lightly browned.
9 Dust with paprika and replace the reserved tops.
10 Place a nest of watercress in the centre of each serving plate, arrange a tomato on top and serve at once.

Serves 8

Equipment
shallow baking dish

NOTES

Add the egg whites immediately before baking. The tomato soufflés cannot be frozen.

This dish can be served at the end of a meal, in the tradition of the English "savoury".

GRILLED MEDITERRANEAN VEGETABLES

CONTRIBUTED BY PRUE LEITH
LEITH'S, LONDON

1 Preheat the grill/broiler or barbecue.

2 Cut the fennel and radicchio into thick slices, leaving some stalk end on each slice to hold the leaves together.

3 In a large bowl, turn all the vegetables in olive oil to coat.

4 Arrange the vegetables on the grill pan, in the grill basket or on a foil-covered grill/broiler tray.

5 Grill slowly at first until the vegetables are soft.

6 Then cook fiercely, turning to char the edges on all sides.

7 Arrange on a heated platter (if you have to cook the vegetables in batches, hold them on this platter in a warm oven until grilling is completed).

8 Serve hot, drizzled with additional olive oil, seasoned generously with sea salt and freshly ground black pepper and garnished with sprigs of fresh basil. (This dish is also delicious served at room temperature.)

9 Have additional sea salt, black pepper and olive oil available at the table.

Serves 4

Equipment
grill/broiler or barbecue with grill
　basket

NOTES

To peel raw bell peppers, first use a swivel peeler to remove as much of the outer membrane as possible. Then cut along the vertical creases to divide the peppers into sections. Using the peeler, remove the remaining membrane at the edges of these sections.

INGREDIENTS

1 head of fennel
1 head of radicchio
1 small aubergine/eggplant – sliced
　lengthways into thin strips
1 courgette/zucchini – sliced
　lengthways into thin strips
4 spring onions/scallions –
　trimmed (sliced in half
　lengthways if thick)
4 field mushrooms – tough stems
　removed and very thickly sliced
1 red and 1 yellow bell pepper –
　peeled, seeded and cut into
　large flat pieces
extra virgin olive oil
sea salt and freshly ground black
　pepper

To garnish
fresh basil leaves

Fresh Pasta with Snail Ragù

CONTRIBUTED BY CHEF ALBERICO PENATI
HARRY'S BAR, LONDON

INGREDIENTS

400g/14oz fresh pasta (preferably home-made)
100g/3½oz (¾ cup) freshly grated Parmesan cheese

For the ragù
6 Tbl olive oil
100g/3½oz (¾ cup) finely chopped shallots
4 Tbl finely chopped celery
60g/2oz (½ cup) finely chopped flat-leaf parsley
2 tsp finely chopped garlic
300g/10½oz tinned snails – cleaned, blanched and drained
120ml/4fl oz (½ cup) dry white wine
240ml/8fl oz (1 cup) vegetable stock
salt and freshly ground black pepper to taste
120ml/4fl oz (½ cup) double/heavy cream
60g/2oz (4 Tbl) butter – cut into bits

To garnish
very finely chopped fresh parsley

Prepare the ragù:
1 Preheat the oven to 180°C/350°F/Gas Mark 4.
2 In an flameproof casserole, heat 3 Tbl of the olive oil and sauté the shallots, celery, parsley and garlic until softened – do not let them colour.
3 Add the snails and white wine.
4 Cook until the liquid has reduced by half, then add the stock and salt and pepper to taste.
5 Cover and place in the oven for 30 minutes.
6 Remove from the oven and, over medium heat, stir in the cream, the remaining 3 Tbl of olive oil and the butter to thicken the sauce – keep warm.

Cook the pasta and serve:
1 Cook the pasta in plenty of boiling salted water.
2 When pasta is al dente (still firm to the bite), drain and add to the ragù.
3 Toss with most of the cheese, check the seasoning and arrange on heated serving plates. Garnish with the remaining cheese and the chopped fresh parsley and serve at once.

Serves 4 to 6

Equipment
flameproof casserole with lid

NOTES

Tinned snails (already cleaned and blanched) are available in speciality shops. Most are produced in France or China. The French are considered superior but are significantly more expensive. The preparation of fresh snails can be time-consuming and complicated and is recommended only for experienced cooks.

GREEN NOODLES AU GRATIN WITH PARMA HAM

CONTRIBUTED BY CHEF RENATO PICCOLOTTA
HOTEL CIPRIANI, VENICE, ITALY

INGREDIENTS

50g/1¾oz (3½ Tbl) butter
100g/3½oz Parma ham – lightly
    blanched and cut into thin
    julienne strips
500g/1lb 2oz thin green noodles,
    home-made or shop bought
150ml/5fl oz (½ cup + 2 Tbl)
    béchamel sauce
150g/5oz (1⅓ cups) freshly grated
    Parmesan cheese
salt and freshly ground black
    pepper to taste

Serve with
a fresh mixed salad

Continued opposite

1 Preheat the grill/broiler and bring a large pot of salted water to a rolling boil.
2 Melt the butter in a large pan, add the ham and cook over high heat until the fat of the ham has dissolved.
3 Cook the noodles in the boiling salted water until al dente (fresh takes only 2–3 minutes; check package directions for shop bought) – quickly drain.
4 Immediately add the cooked pasta to the ham and butter mixture. Toss and season with freshly ground black pepper.
5 Gently mix in a little of the béchamel sauce (or, if you prefer, use a little cream to coat the pasta at this point).
6 Place the mixture in an ovenproof serving dish, cover with the remaining béchamel sauce and sprinkle with Parmesan.
7 Place under the hot grill/broiler for a few minutes, just until the surface is lightly golden.
8 Serve immediately on heated plates.

Serves 6

Equipment
pasta machine or rolling pin –
    if making your own noodles
ovenproof serving dish

NOTES

The béchamel sauce recipe is given opposite, as too is the method for making your own green pasta noodles.

140

To make the noodles:

1 Pour the flour on to a work surface and shape into a mound, making a hollow in the centre.

2 Break the eggs into the hollow together with the spinach and salt.

3 Using a fork, mix the flour into the egg and spinach.

4 Form into a ball, cover with clingfilm/plastic wrap and let rest for approximately 2 hours in a cool place.

5 Using a pasta machine or rolling pin, roll out the dough as thinly as possible. Let it dry for approximately 10 minutes (until it has a soft leathery texture) then roll it loosely into a flat tube.

6 With a sharp knife, cut the roll into very thin strips. Unravel the strips and heap them on a tray until you are ready to use them.

To make the béchamel sauce:

1 Place the milk, nutmeg and pepper in a saucepan, bring to a simmer, lower the heat and let steep for 10 minutes.

2 In a heavy-bottomed saucepan, melt the butter and stir in the flour to make a roux. Stirring constantly, cook for 1 minute without letting it colour.

3 Remove the roux from the heat and, whisking constantly, gradually add the milk to it.

4 Return the sauce to the heat and, whisking constantly, bring to the boil, simmer for 3 minutes, check seasonings and remove from heat.

When making béchamel sauce, avoid using aluminium utensils.

INGREDIENTS

For the noodles
400g/14oz (3½ cups) plain/all purpose flour
3 eggs (medium or large)
100g/3½oz (½ cup) cooked spinach – squeezed dry and chopped
a pinch of salt

To make 150ml/5fl oz (½ cup + 2 Tbl) of béchamel sauce:
150ml/5fl oz (½ cup + 2 Tbl) creamy milk
small pinch of nutmeg
a grind of white pepper
15g/½ oz (1 Tbl) butter
15g/½ oz (2 Tbl) plain/all purpose flour

OPEN RAVIOLI WITH ARTICHOKES, ASPARAGUS AND DUBLIN BAY PRAWNS

CONTRIBUTED BY CHEF DOMINIQUE LE STANC
RESTAURANT LE CHANTECLER, HOTEL NEGRESCO, NICE, FRANCE

INGREDIENTS

12 fresh green asparagus spears
18 uncooked Dublin Bay prawn
  tails — shelled
2 Tbl extra virgin olive oil plus
  1 Tbl for frying the vegetables
1 sprig fresh thyme
12 small fresh artichoke hearts
  — sliced
salt and freshly ground black
  pepper to taste

For the ravioli dough
300g/10½oz (2¼ cups) plain/all
  purpose flour
3 eggs — at room temperature
2 tsp olive oil

To garnish
fresh flat-leaf parsley

Make the ravioli dough:
1 In a large bowl, mix the flour, eggs and olive oil into a smooth dough using your hands.
2 Rest the dough in the refrigerator for at least 1 hour.
3 On a lightly floured surface, roll out the dough very thinly and cut into 12 rectangles of 8 x 12cm/3 x 5in.

Prepare the ingredients:
1 While the dough is resting, boil the asparagus in salted water for 7–10 minutes, rinse immediately under cold water, drain and cut into small sections — reserve.
2 Preheat the oven to 200°C/400°F/Gas Mark 6.
3 Prepare a large pan of lightly salted water in which to boil the pasta.
4 Prepare the prawns by placing them on a lightly oiled baking tray.
5 In a small bowl combine the 2 Tbl of extra virgin olive oil with the leaves from the sprig of thyme — reserve.
6 In a frying pan, heat the remaining 1 Tbl of olive oil, add the sliced artichoke hearts and fry until heated through.
7 Add the asparagus and season to taste.
8 Place the prawns in the oven to bake for 2–3 minutes.
9 Meanwhile boil the pasta for about 1 minute — drain.

Quickly assemble the dish:
1 Divide the thyme and olive oil among 6 heated soup plates.
2 Arrange one piece of ravioli in the middle of each plate.
3 Top with the prawns and vegetables.
4 Cover with a second piece of pasta.
5 Garnish with parsley and serve at once.

Serves 6

Equipment
baking tray/sheet — oiled

NOTES

Ravioli Ouverts aux Artichauts, Pointes d'Asperges et Langoustines (French)

To prepare artichoke hearts, first slice off the stem of the artichoke with a sharp knife. Cut off the large bottom leaves and trim the base of any remaining green. Slice off the cone of soft leaves. Cut the base into quarters, and trim off and discard the fuzzy choke. Rub the pieces with lemon and place in cold water until needed.

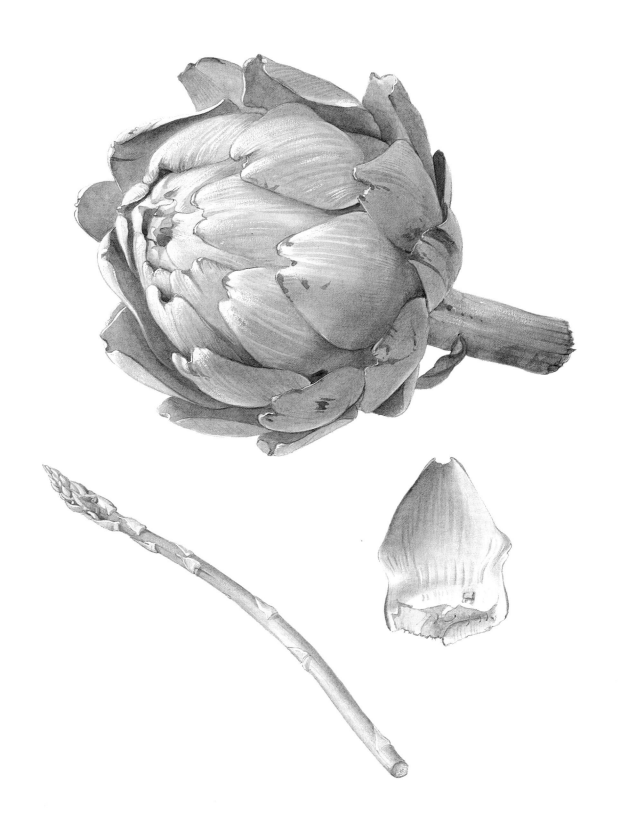

CRAB TORTELLI WITH YOUNG MARROW

CONTRIBUTED BY HOTEL HASSLER, ROME, ITALY

INGREDIENTS

For the pasta
400g/14oz (3½ cups) plain/all
    purpose flour
3 eggs
1 Tbl olive oil

For the stuffing
300g/10½oz white crab meat –
    carefully picked over
100g/3½oz (1¼ cups) fresh
    breadcrumbs
2 Tbl finely chopped parsley
1 clove garlic – finely chopped
50g/1¾oz (⅔ cup) freshly grated
    Parmesan cheese

For the sauce
5 young marrow/zucchini squash
    with blossoms – roughly
    chopped
1 clove garlic – finely chopped
235ml/8fl oz (1 cup) stock
    (chicken or vegetable)
2 Tbl double/heavy cream
1 Tbl finely chopped flat-leaf
    parsley
100g/3½oz (⅔ cup) freshly grated
    Parmesan cheese
salt and freshly ground white
    pepper to taste

1 Combine the pasta ingredients in a large bowl using your hands, knead until they form a smooth dough, cover with a damp cloth and leave to rest for 30 minutes.
2 Meanwhile, in a large bowl, combine all the stuffing ingredients – reserve.
3 On a lightly floured surface, roll out the dough until almost paper thin and cut into 5cm/2in squares.
4 Place a bit of stuffing in the centre of each pasta square then, moistening the edges, close the pasta over the filling to form a triangle. Press the edges firmly together to seal and reserve, covered with a slightly damp tea towel.

Prepare the sauce:
1 In a bowl, combine the squash and garlic.
2 In a saucepan, bring the stock to the boil.
3 Add the squash mixture and cook over high heat until the broth has evaporated.
4 Add the cream and season with salt and freshly ground pepper to taste.

Cook the pasta and serve:
1 Cook the pasta in a large pan of gently simmering lightly salted water for 3–5 mins (do not overcook).
2 Drain the cooked pasta – gently toss with the sauce to coat.
3 Season with remaining parsley and Parmesan cheese.
4 Serve immediately on heated plates.

Serves 4 to 6

NOTES

Young marrow/zucchini squash with their bright golden blossoms are extremely perishable but are sometimes available in speciality markets in the early spring. The blossoms should be gently but thoroughly washed, inside and out, under cold water, then dried on kitchen paper. If blossoming squash are unavailable, use a combination of green and yellow summer squash.

FETTUCCINE WITH ASPARAGUS, ARTICHOKE AND SWEET PEPPERS

CONTRIBUTED BY JOE'S, LONDON

Serves 6 to 8

1 Cook the fettuccine in plenty of salted boiling water until al dente — drain and refresh in cold water.
2 Meanwhile, in a large saucepan, melt the butter. Add the shallots and sweat until softened but not browned.
3 Deglaze with white wine and vegetable stock and reduce by half.
4 Add the double cream and reduce the sauce until it coats the back of a metal spoon. Season to taste.

To serve the dish:
1 In a large pan, sauté the prepared vegetables in the olive oil.
2 Plunge the fettuccine into boiling water and instantly drain it.
3 Add the hot pasta to the vegetables.
4 Add the sauce and mix well.
5 Season and serve immediately on heated plates, garnished with chopped fresh herbs. Pass freshly grated Parmesan cheese separately.

INGREDIENTS

900g/2lb fresh fettuccine
1 Tbl butter
2 large shallots — finely chopped
300ml/10fl oz (1¼ cups) dry white wine
300ml/10fl oz (1¼ cups) vegetable stock
300ml/10fl oz (1¼ cups) double/heavy cream
450g/1lb green asparagus — peeled, blanched and cut into 2.5cm/1in pieces
450g/1lb red bell peppers roasted, skinned, seeded and cut into 2.5cm/1in strips
1 large globe artichoke — trimmed to the heart, blanched until soft and cut into thin strips
2 Tbl olive oil
salt and freshly ground white pepper to taste

To garnish
a combination of chopped fresh chervil, chives and parsley
freshly grated Parmesan cheese

NOTES

Globe artichokes are the immature flowers of a member of the thistle family. They consist of tightly overlapping thorn-topped leaves, an inedible hairy choke, a fleshly heart and an edible stem. Artichokes come in a number of types and sizes; the small purple variety from Provence is so tender it is eaten whole and raw, while the large Brittany ones can weigh close to 1 lb (450g) and must be steamed or boiled until tender.

Choose ones with firm, tightly closed leaves. Store fresh artichokes like the flowers they are: trim off a bit of the stem and stand in fresh water in a cool place or refrigerator. Globe artichokes are not even remotely related to Jerusalem artichokes, which are the edible underground tubers of a variety of sunflower plant.

FETTUCCINE WITH SMOKED CHICKEN AND MUSTARD SAGE SAUCE

....

CONTRIBUTED BY CHEF DAVID BASTIDE
VENTICELLO RISTORANTE, SAN FRANCISCO, USA

INGREDIENTS

....

1 smoked chicken (or 2 smoked
   chicken breasts)
2 Tbl olive oil
115g/4oz (1 cup) chopped onion
225g/8oz (1 cup) chopped carrots
2 sticks celery – chopped
2 cloves garlic – unpeeled
1.5 litres/2½ pints (6 cups) chicken
   stock
175g/6oz (12 Tbl) unsalted butter
175g/6oz (1½ cups) plain/all
   purpose flour
30g/1oz bunch of sage
2 Tbl Dijon mustard
120ml/4fl oz (½ cup) double/heavy
   cream
900g/2lb fresh fettuccine
salt and freshly ground white
   pepper to taste

To garnish
lemon wedges

Serves 8

1 Skin, bone and dice the chicken meat – cover and set aside (reserve bones and trimmings).

2 In a large saucepan, heat the oil, add the onion, carrot and celery and lightly brown.

3 Smash and add the unpeeled garlic cloves to the saucepan along with the reserved bones and trimmings.

4 Add 1.2 litres/2 pints (5 cups) of the chicken stock (reserving the remainder for thinning the sauce if necessary).

5 Simmer, uncovered, until reduced by approximately half.

6 Put a large pot of lightly salted water on to boil for the fettuccine.

7 Meanwhile, in another saucepan, melt the butter and, stirring constantly, add the flour. Cook for 5 minutes over low heat to make a roux, stirring continuously but not allowing the roux to colour.

8 Pick out several of the nicest sage leaves for garnish and reserve – tear and bruise the remaining leaves and add them along with their stems to the reduced stock mixture.

9 Stir the roux into the stock and simmer over low heat for 5–7 minutes.

10 Strain the stock into a clean saucepan (discarding the solids).

11 Whisk the mustard and cream into the stock (do not allow to boil).

12 Cook the fettuccine in the boiling salted water until al dente.

13 Meanwhile, add the diced chicken to the sauce (if desired it may be thinned by adding additional stock or thickened by allowing it to reduce further) and season to taste.

14 Drain the pasta well and arrange on a large warm serving dish. Pour the sauce over, garnish with fresh sage leaves and lemon wedges and serve immediately.

THAI FRIED NOODLES

CONTRIBUTED BY CHEF VATCHARIN BHUMICHITR
CHIANG MAI RESTAURANT, LONDON

INGREDIENTS

120g/4oz dry sen lek noodles
3 Tbl oil (groundnut/peanut or
   vegetable)
1 clove garlic – finely chopped
60g/2oz ready-fried beancurd
   (tofu) – cut into 1cm/½in cubes
1 egg
1 Tbl finely chopped preserved
   turnip (chi po)
2 spring onions/scallions – cut into
   2.5cm/1in pieces
2 Tbl roughly chopped roasted
   peanuts
90g/3oz (1½ cups) fresh bean
   sprouts
½ tsp chilli powder
1 tsp caster/superfine sugar
2 Tbl light soy sauce
1 Tbl fresh lemon juice

To garnish
sprigs of fresh coriander/cilantro –
   coarsely chopped
2 lemon wedges
"Four Flavours" accompaniments

1 Soak the noodles in a bowl of cold water for 20 minutes until soft. Drain and reserve.
2 In a wok (or frying pan), heat the oil until a light haze appears.
3 Add the garlic and fry until golden brown.
4 Add the beancurd cubes and stir briefly.
5 Break the egg into the wok, cook for a moment, then stir.
6 Add the noodles and stir well.
7 Add the preserved turnip, spring onion, half of the peanuts and half of the bean sprouts and stir well.
8 Add the chilli powder, sugar, soy sauce and lemon juice and cook, stirring well, until the liquid is absorbed and the noodles are tender.
9 Turn the dish out on to serving plates and sprinkle with remaining peanuts and the chopped coriander leaves.
10 Arrange the lemon wedges and the remaining bean sprouts (to be mixed in by each person at the last moment) on the side of each plate and serve at once along with a side dish of the "Four Flavours".

Serves 2

Equipment
wok or large frying pan

NOTES

Gueyteow Pad Thai

Sen lek (rice stick) noodles are flat rice noodles about 2mm wide. They are available in most oriental markets, usually dry.

Preserved turnip (chi po), often labelled sweetened turnip, is one of a wide variety of pickles available in oriental markets. It is usually used finely chopped and in small amounts to add flavour to dishes.

The "Four Flavours" are nam tan (sugar), nam prik pla (fish sauce with chopped chillies), prik nam som (vinegar with chopped chillies) and prik pon (red chilli powder). They are available in a pack from oriental markets and some supermarkets.

Ready-fried beancurd is a block of fresh white tofu that has been fried until golden yellow on the outside. Its firm texture makes it especially suitable for stir-fries.

PENNE WITH TOMATO, CREAM AND FIVE CHEESES

CONTRIBUTED BY CHEFS JOHANNE KILLEEN AND GEORGE GERMON
AL FORNO, PROVIDENCE, RHODE ISLAND, USA

1 Preheat the oven to 240°C/475°F/Gas Mark 9.

2 In a stockpot, bring 4.7 litres/8 pints (20 cups) of salted water to the boil.

3 In a large bowl, combine all the sauce ingredients and stir well.

4 Parboil the pasta for 4 minutes then drain.

5 Add the pasta to the sauce ingredients and toss well.

6 Place the pasta mixture in the gratin dish or dishes, dot with small pieces of the butter and bake until bubbly and brown (approximately 7–10 minutes).

7 Serve immediately.

Serves 6 to 8

Equipment
6–8 individual shallow gratin dishes or 1 large shallow gratin dish

INGREDIENTS

450g/1lb dried penne rigate pasta
60g/2oz (4 Tbl) unsalted butter

For the sauce
470ml/16fl oz (2 cups) double/heavy cream
225g/8oz (1 cup) chopped tinned tomatoes (packed in purée)
45g/1½oz (½ cup) freshly grated Pecorino Romano cheese
45g/1½oz (½ cup) coarsely shredded fontina cheese
45g/1½oz (4 Tbl) crumbled Gorgonzola cheese
2 Tbl ricotta cheese
115g/4oz fresh mozzarella cheese – sliced
¾ tsp kosher or coarse sea salt
6 fresh basil leaves – chopped

To garnish
small sprigs of fresh basil

Serve with
Italian bread

NOTES

Adapted from Cucina Simpatica, HarperCollins, New York, 1991.

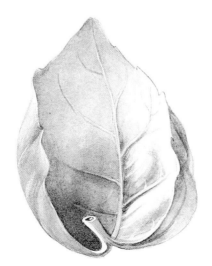

PUDDINGS

HOT PEAR SOUFFLÉ

....

CONTRIBUTED BY CHEF MAIR LEWIS
BODYSGALLEN HALL HOTEL, GWYNEDD, WALES

INGREDIENTS

For the apricot sauce
900g/2lb apricots (fresh or dried)
500ml/17fl oz (2 cups + 1 Tbl)
   water
225g/8oz (1 cup) caster/superfine
   sugar
1 vanilla pod/bean
½ lemon

For the pear soufflés
5 well-ripened pears (each
   approximately 120g/4oz)
½ lemon
60g/2oz (¼ cup) caster/superfine
   sugar
1½ Tbl Poire William liqueur
5 egg yolks
12 egg whites
a pinch of salt
2 Tbl icing/confectioners' sugar –
   optional

For the stock syrup
1 litre/34fl oz (4¼ cups) water
100g/3½oz (a scant ½ cup)
   caster/superfine sugar
1 vanilla pod split lengthways –
   optional
½ lemon

Continued opposite

First make the apricot sauce:

1 Place the ingredients except for the apricots in a saucepan and bring to the boil.

2 Strain the syrup into a clean pan and keep warm.

3 Remove the stones from fresh apricots, if using.

4 Place the apricots in a saucepan with a very small amount of water and cook until very soft – cool slightly.

5 Rub the cooked apricot purée through a sieve into a clean pan, return to the heat and begin to add the warm syrup slowly.

6 Continue to add syrup until the sauce has a light, free-running consistency (the amount of syrup needed varies depending on how thick the apricot purée is after it has been sieved).

7 Set the apricot syrup aside, keeping warm.

Prepare the soufflé ingredients:

1 Place all the stock syrup ingredients in a large saucepan and bring to the boil.

2 Meanwhile, peel and core the pears, rub them with the lemon half and cut into quarters.

3 Cook the pears in the boiling stock for 15 minutes then drain.

4 Place the warm pears, caster sugar, Poire William and egg yolks in a blender or food processor and blend for 1 minute.

5 Transfer the mixture to a large bowl – keep warm but not hot.

6 Preheat the oven to 220°C/425°F/Gas Mark 7.

Serves 6

Equipment
6 individual ramekins (about
   9 × 6cm/3½ × 2½in)
blender or food processor
sieve

NOTES

Soufflés should be served as soon as possible because they tend to deflate quickly. A good soufflé, however, will stand for 2 or 3 minutes.

Prepare the soufflé moulds:

1 Brush the interior of the dishes lightly but thoroughly with soft butter.

2 Sprinkle with sugar.

3 Turn the moulds upside down and tap the base to dislodge any surplus sugar.

Finish the soufflés, bake and serve:

1 In a large dry bowl, beat the egg whites until they stand in soft peaks (do not over-beat). Towards the end of the operation, incorporate the icing sugar, beating all the time. You should now have a thick, glossy meringue.

2 Take a quarter of the egg whites and, using a spoon in figure eight movements, mix carefully into the pear mixture.

3 Using a metal spoon, gradually fold in the remaining egg whites, lifting the mixture lightly to keep it airy (do not over-mix).

4 Fill the soufflé dishes to the top and level the surface with the side of a metal spatula. With your thumb, push the mixture away from the edge of each dish to enable the soufflés to rise more easily.

5 Place the soufflés on a baking tray and bake for approximately 10 minutes (this could take a bit longer – perhaps 12–14 minutes). After 5 minutes the soufflés should begin to rise: check that they are rising evenly, and if not free the edges with a knife.

6 Meanwhile, bring the apricot sauce to the boil – it should be served hot.

7 When the soufflés are cooked, serve as soon as possible, passing the apricot sauce separately.

When you check the soufflés after 5 minutes, you may dust each one with a little icing sugar to produce a caramelized glaze.

INGREDIENTS

For preparing the soufflé moulds
20g/¾oz (1½ Tbl) butter – soft
30g/1oz (2 Tbl) caster/superfine
  sugar

Serve with
light fruit sorbet, home-made
  ice cream, Chantilly cream,
  warm chocolate sauce or crisp
  tuile biscuits

BITTER-SWEET CHOCOLATE SORBET

CONTRIBUTED BY CHEZ NICO AT NINETY, LONDON

1 Over a saucepan, rub the sugar cubes against the skin of the orange to absorb its essential oils and flavour (reserve the orange for another use).

2 Place the sugar cubes in the saucepan along with the caster sugar and water, and heat until the sugar dissolves. Bring to the boil.

3 Place the cocoa and chocolate in a bowl and pour the boiling sugar syrup over them, whisking to incorporate all the ingredients.

4 Pass the mixture through a fine sieve – cool.

5 Place the cooled mixture in an ice-cream maker and churn until you have thick ribbons of sorbet on the surface.

6 Cover and place in the freezer for 6 hours.

7 Serve spoonfuls of sorbet on individual plates garnished with fresh orange segments.

INGREDIENTS

75g/2½oz (⅓ cup) sugar cubes
1 orange – washed and dried
100g/3½oz (½ cup)
   caster/superfine sugar
400ml/14fl oz (1¾ cups) water
80g/2¾oz (¾ cup) cocoa powder
100g/3½oz bitter-sweet chocolate
   – roughly chopped

To garnish
fresh orange segments

Serves 10

Equipment
ice-cream maker
fine sieve/chinois

NOTES

The sorbet keeps for a week in the freezer. Defrost and churn again before reusing.

CHOCOLATE BREAD AND BUTTER PUDDING

CONTRIBUTED BY CHEF JASPER WHITE
BOSTON, MASSACHUSETTS, USA

INGREDIENTS

120g/4oz plain/semi-sweet
   chocolate – chopped into small
   pieces
350ml/12fl oz (1½ cups)
   double/heavy cream
350ml/12fl oz (1½ cups) milk
⅛ tsp salt
6 egg yolks
120g/4oz (½ cup) granulated sugar
½ tsp vanilla essence
1 day-old French baguette
90g/3oz (6 Tbl) unsalted butter

To garnish
a custard sauce, berry purée,
   hot chocolate sauce or
   double/heavy cream

1 In a saucepan over low temperature, heat the chocolate, cream, milk and salt, stirring often until the chocolate has completely melted.

2 In a large bowl, combine the egg yolks, sugar and vanilla.

3 Gradually whisk the chocolate cream into the egg mixture – set aside.

4 Cut the bread into 8cm/3in sections and square off the sections by removing the crust.

5 Slice each section lengthways into pieces no more than 1cm/½in thick.

6 In a small pan, melt the butter.

7 Lightly brush the baking dish with the melted butter. Brush both sides of each piece of bread with butter and arrange in the baking dish in neat rows, slightly overlapping for a shingled effect.

8 When the dish is full, gently pour the custard over the bread – allow to sit for at least 30 minutes (pushing down on the bread occasionally so that it absorbs the custard).

9 Meanwhile, preheat the oven to 170°C/325°F/Gas Mark 3 and place a large pan of water on to boil.

10 Place the pudding in a baking tin and fill the tin with enough boiling water to come halfway up the sides of the pudding dish.

11 Bake for 30 minutes or until set around the edges but still a little "nervous" in the centre.

12 Allow to cool for at least 15 minutes. Cut the pudding into squares and serve it garnished with cream, a dessert sauce or fruit purée.

Serves 6 to 8

Equipment
18 x 28cm/7 x 11in baking dish
baking tin/pan large enough to
   hold the baking dish in a
   water bath

NOTES

Adapted from Jasper White's
Cooking From New England,
Harper and Row, 1989.

CHOCOLATE POTS WITH PRESERVED ORANGE PEEL

CONTRIBUTED BY CHEF JEAN-YVES MOREL

MOREL'S, HASLEMERE, SURREY, ENGLAND

1 Preheat the oven to 180°C/350°F/Gas Mark 4 and place a large pan of water on to boil.

2 In a heavy-bottomed saucepan, bring the cream to the boil.

3 Add the chocolate pieces and stir until incorporated.

4 Pour into a blender or food processor and blend until smooth, adding the egg during processing.

5 Add the preserved orange pieces.

6 Pour the mixture into 6 small ramekins.

7 Arrange the ramekins in a baking tin and fill the tin with enough boiling water water to come halfway up the sides of the ramekins. Bake for 15–20 minutes.

8 Remove from the oven and leave to cool.

9 Cover each cooled pot with clingfilm and refrigerate for several hours or overnight.

10 Serve chilled, garnished with whipped cream and a few pieces of preserved orange peel.

Serves 6

Equipment
food processor or blender
6 individual ramekins
baking tin/pan large enough to
    hold the ramekins in a
    water bath
clingfilm/plastic wrap

INGREDIENTS

300ml/10fl oz (1¼ cups)
    single/light cream
200g/7oz bitter chocolate –
    broken into small pieces
1 egg
100g/3½oz (¾ cup) preserved
    orange peel – chopped

To garnish
small dabs of whipped cream
a little preserved orange peel

NOTES

The pots should not be frozen.

Crisp tuile biscuits are an ideal accompaniment.

SUMMER PUDDING

....

CONTRIBUTED BY LISA DAVIDSON, OXFORDSHIRE, ENGLAND

INGREDIENTS

450g/1lb (4 cups) raspberries
225g/8oz (2 cups) redcurrants or
  blueberries
115g/4oz (1 cup) blackcurrants
140g/5oz (⅔ cup) caster/superfine
  sugar
7 or 8 medium slices of stale
  white bread, crusts removed

To garnish
a few reserved "perfect" berries
fresh mint sprigs

Serve with
double/heavy cream

1 Wash and carefully pick over the fruit, removing stems and any berries that look "musty".
2 Place the fruit and sugar in a large saucepan and cook over medium heat just until the sugar melts and the juices begin to run (3 to 5 minutes) — be careful not to overcook or you will lose the fresh taste of the berries.
3 Remove the fruit from the heat.
4 Ladle 300ml/10fl oz (1¼ cups) of juice from the fruit — reserve.
5 Line the sides and bottom of the buttered pudding basin with slightly overlapping slices of bread, reserving some for the top. Seal well by pressing the edges together, and fill any gaps with small pieces of bread so that no juice can escape.
6 Place the fruit in the lined basin.
7 Cover the fruit with a final slice of bread using additional odd bits to cover any gaps and making sure the edges are sealed together.
8 Put the plate on top of the bread, and the weights on top of this, and refrigerate the weighted-down pudding overnight. Refrigerate the reserved juice too.
9 Just before serving, turn the pudding out on to a serving plate and pour the reserved fruit juice over any remaining white bits of bread. Decorate with reserved berries and mint sprigs.
10 Serve by cutting the pudding into slices and topping each serving with lashings of fresh cream.

Serves 8

Equipment
1½ pints/4 cups pudding basin —
  lightly buttered
plate that fits exactly into the rim
  of the basin
1½ or 2 kg/3 or 4 lbs of kitchen
  weights

NOTES

A few food tins will do as weights.

LIME MOUSSELINE AND SESAME BISCUITS

CONTRIBUTED BY LADY WEINBERG (ANOUSKA HEMPEL)
BLAKES HOTEL, LONDON

INGREDIENTS

For the lime mousseline
235ml/8fl oz (1 cup) milk
4 Tbl caster/superfine sugar
5 egg yolks
3 Tbl grated lime zest (the zest of
   7 limes – be careful to avoid the
   bitter white pith)
2½ leaves of gelatin or 2½ tsp
   gelatin powder
235ml/8fl oz (1 cup) double/heavy
   cream
235ml/8fl oz (1 cup) fresh lime
   juice (the juice of 7 limes)

For the sesame biscuits
3 Tbl orange zest (the zest of
   3 oranges)
255g/9oz (1 cup + 2 Tbl)
   caster/superfine sugar
120ml/4fl oz (½ cup) fresh orange
   juice
125g/4½oz black sesame seeds
200g/7oz (1½ cup) plain/all
   purpose flour – sifted
125g/4½oz butter – melted

Prepare the lime mousseline:
1 In a saucepan, bring the milk and sugar to the boil.
2 Lower the heat and, one at a time, whisk in the egg yolks.
Continue whisking until foamy but without allowing the
mixture to boil.
3 Add the lime zest and infuse over low heat for 2 minutes.
4 Meanwhile soften the gelatin leaves in cold water for 2
minutes. Gently wring them out and add to the hot mixture.
If using powdered gelatin, soften it in 2 Tbl of water for 5
minutes then add to the mixture.
5 Whisk to incorporate the softened gelatin, remove the
mixture from the heat, pass through a fine sieve and allow to
cool.
6 Meanwhile, in a cold bowl, whip the cream.
7 When the lime mixture is cool, gently fold in the whipped
cream alternately with the lime juice.
8 Pour into the individual ramekins or the pudding bowl and
chill until ready to serve (at least 3 hours).

Prepare the sesame biscuits:
1 In a bowl, combine the orange zest, sugar and orange juice.
2 Mix in the sesame seeds and flour.
3 Thoroughly mix in the melted butter.
4 Allow to rest (covered, at room temperature) for 2–3 hours.
5 Preheat the oven to 150°C/300°F/Gas Mark 2.
6 Spread the batter very thinly (in desired shapes) on the
greased baking trays and bake until golden (about 10 minutes).
7 Quickly, while they are still warm, mould the biscuits into
desired shapes by bending them over a rolling pin, rolling them
into "cigarettes", or forming them into "baskets" over the
bottom of an inverted cup. Serve on the side of the chilled
lime mousseline.

Serves 8

Equipment
fine sieve/chinois
baking tray/sheet/s – greased
8 individual ramekins or 1 pudding
   bowl

NOTES

Thin plastic templates are available
in speciality cooking shops to give
fancy shapes to spread biscuit
batter. Cutting the desired shape
out of a piece of thin cardboard
will also do the trick.

KISSEL

CONTRIBUTED BY PRINCESS GEORGE GALITZINE, LONDON

Serves 4 to 6

Equipment
fine sieve/chinois

1 Wash and carefully pick over the fruit, removing stems and bruised or damaged parts, and reserving any perfect berries for the garnish.

2 Combine the fruit and sugar with 450ml/15fl oz (1¾ cups + 2 Tbl) of the water in a pan and bring to the boil over medium heat.

3 Rub the fruit purée through a fine sieve and return to the pan. Set aside, off the heat.

4 In a small bowl, stir the cornflour into the remaining 150ml/5fl oz (½ cup + 2 Tbl) water until smooth.

5 Add the cornflour mixture to the fruit, return the pan to medium heat and cook until the mixture has the consistency of a thick, smooth sauce.

6 Pour into a serving bowl and chill for several hours.

7 Serve garnished with single cream, reserved berries and mint leaves.

INGREDIENTS

450g/1lb (3 cups) berries such as
    raspberries or blackberries
4 rounded Tbl caster/superfine
    sugar
1 rounded Tbl
    cornflour/cornstarch
600ml/1 pint (2½ cups) water

To garnish
single/light cream
mint leaves and reserved berries

NOTES

Small biscuits such as amaretti are ideal to serve with kissel.

GINGER ICE CREAM

CONTRIBUTED BY ADMIRAL SIR BENJAMIN AND LADY BATHURST, ENGLAND

INGREDIENTS

175g/6oz (¾ cup) caster/superfine sugar

150ml/5fl oz (½ cup + 2 Tbl) fresh lemon juice (approximately 3 lemons)

1 tsp powdered gelatin

1 Tbl water

2 large egg whites

a pinch of salt

300ml/10fl oz (1¼ cups) double/heavy cream

60g/2oz (⅓ cup) crystallized ginger or to taste – finely chopped

To garnish
grated chocolate
slivered crystallized ginger

1 In a saucepan over low heat, dissolve the sugar in the lemon juice, stirring constantly.

2 Place the gelatin in a cup with the water and place this cup in a bowl of boiling water until the gelatin dissolves.

3 Add the gelatin to the lemon mixture, bring to the boil and let bubble fiercely for 3 minutes.

4 Meanwhile, in a large clean bowl, whip the egg whites with the salt until stiff.

5 In a thin stream, pour the lemon mixture into the egg whites, whisking hard all the time. Continue whisking until cool and thick.

6 In a separate bowl, whisk the cream until thick.

7 Fold the cream and the ginger into the egg white and lemon mixture, pour into the container/s and freeze.

8 Serve straight from the freezer, garnished with grated chocolate or slivers of ginger.

Serves 6 to 8

Equipment
6 to 8 individual ramekins or 1 large freezer-proof container

NOTES

For a variation, replace the crystallized ginger in the ice cream with 200g/7oz plain or minty chocolate bars that have been finely chopped in a food processor.

This recipe is perfect for using up leftover egg whites – which can be frozen in small containers or ice-cube trays for later use.

GINGER VACHERIN

CONTRIBUTED BY CLAIRE MACDONALD, THE LADY MACDONALD
KINLOCH LODGE HOTEL, ISLE OF SKYE, SCOTLAND

INGREDIENTS

5 large egg whites
285g/10oz (1¼ cups)
    caster/superfine sugar
2 tsp ground ginger

For the filling
450ml/15fl oz (1¾ cups + 2 Tbl)
    double/heavy cream
preserved ginger in syrup: 2 Tbl
    syrup, and 6 pieces of ginger –
    chopped

To garnish
sieved icing/confectioners' sugar

1 Preheat the oven to 125°C/250°F/Gas Mark 1.
2 In a clean, dry bowl, whisk the egg whites until very stiff.
3 Whisking all the time, gradually add the sugar, a spoonful at a time, until completely incorporated.
4 With a large metal spoon, fold in the ground ginger.
5 Take the 2 baking trays and, pencilling around a large plate, trace a circle on the parchment lining each one.
6 Divide the meringue between these 2 circles and smooth evenly.
7 Bake for approximately 2 to 3 hours: they are done when they lift off the parchment cleanly. Cool on a wire rack.
8 Prepare the filling: in a large bowl, whip the cream. Whip in the ginger syrup and fold in the pieces of ginger.
9 Sandwich the meringues together with the filling.
10 Dust the top of the cake with sieved icing sugar and serve as soon as possible.

Serves 8 to 10

Equipment
electric whisk/beater or mixer
2 baking trays/sheets – covered
    with parchment paper

NOTES

Warm dark chocolate sauce or a fresh fruit salad makes a good accompaniment to this pudding.

RICH BANANA ICE CREAM

CONTRIBUTED BY JOSCELINE DIMBLEBY, LONDON

Serves 12

Equipment
electric whisk/beater

1 In a bowl, whisk the eggs and salt until frothy — set aside.
2 In a heavy-bottomed saucepan over low heat, dissolve the sugar in the water and then bring to the boil.
3 Boil the sugar mixture fiercely for 3 minutes, without stirring.
4 Immediately pour this bubbling syrup in a thin stream on to the eggs, whisking all the time with an electric whisk on its fastest setting. Add the cardamom (if using) and continue whisking until the mixture thickens — allow to cool slightly.
5 In another bowl, mash the bananas to a pulp with the lemon juice. Stir this mixture into the eggs and sugar.
6 In a clean bowl, whisk the cream until thick but not stiff and add to the mixture, stirring thoroughly.
7 Pour into a dish, cover and freeze.
8 Serve soon after removing from the freezer, garnished with slivers of toasted almonds.

INGREDIENTS

3 large eggs
½ tsp salt
175g/6oz (1 cup) demerara/light brown sugar
6 Tbl water
a pinch of ground cardamom — optional
4 bananas
juice of 1 fresh lemon
235ml/8fl oz (1 cup) double/heavy cream

To garnish
slivers of toasted almonds

NOTES

Adapted from Josceline Dimbleby's Book of Puddings, Desserts and Savouries, Pan.

Toast whole skinned almonds briefly under a hot grill or in a dry frying pan over medium heat, shaking the grill/frying pan every few seconds to ensure they are evenly toasted. Allow to cool then cut or grate into slivers.

Serve light biscuits or cookies on the side if desired.

BANANA BREAD

CONTRIBUTED BY JANE ASHER, LONDON

INGREDIENTS

90g/3oz (6 Tbl) softened butter

175g/6oz (¾ cup) caster/superfine
sugar

2 large eggs

285g/10oz bananas
(approximately 4) – peeled,
sliced and mashed

225g/8oz (2 cups) plain/all
purpose flour

3 tsp baking powder

60g/2oz (½ cup) chopped walnuts

1 Preheat the oven to 150°C/300°F/Gas Mark 2.

2 In a large bowl, cream the butter and sugar well.

3 Slowly beat in the eggs.

4 Add the banana.

5 In a separate bowl, sieve the flour and baking powder together.

6 Fold the flour mixture into the banana mixture and stir in the walnuts.

7 Turn the mixture into the prepared loaf tin.

8 Bake for 75 minutes or until a wooden skewer or cocktail stick inserted into the middle of the loaf comes out clean.

9 Allow to cool slightly before removing from the tin, then finish cooling on a wire rack.

10 Slice and serve warm or cool – just as it is or spread with butter.

Serves 6 to 8

Equipment
loaf tin/pan – greased and floured

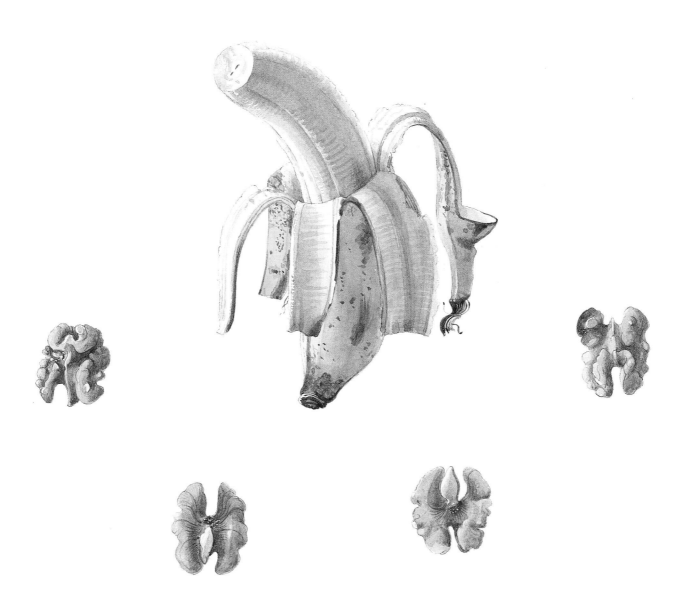

BITTER CHOCOLATE AND ALMOND TORTE

CONTRIBUTED BY CHEFS RUTH ROGERS AND ROSE GRAY
RIVER CAFÉ, LONDON

INGREDIENTS

225g/8oz (1¾ cups) blanched
    almonds
200g/7oz bitter/unsweetened
    chocolate – broken into small
    pieces
225g/8oz (1 cup) unsalted butter
300g/10 ½oz (1⅓ cups)
    caster/superfine sugar
4 large eggs – separated

To garnish
crème fraîche

1 Arrange a shelf one third of the way up the oven and preheat the oven to 150°C/300°F/Gas Mark 2.

2 In a food processor, blender or nut grinder, grind the almonds and chocolate to a fine powder – set aside.

3 Using an electric mixer, cream the butter and beat in the sugar.

4 One at a time, add the egg yolks and beat to mix.

5 Add the ground nuts and chocolate and beat at low speed to mix – set aside.

6 In a separate bowl, beat the egg whites until they form firm peaks.

7 Stir ¼ of the egg whites into the chocolate mixture to lighten it.

8 Gently fold in the remaining egg whites until just blended. Pour into the prepared tin, smooth the top and bake for 45 minutes.

9 Remove from the oven and place the torte, in its tin, on a rack to cool until tepid.

10 Remove from the tin, place on a serving dish and let stand at room temperature. Serve garnished with crème fraîche.

Serves 8 to 10

Equipment
22cm/8½in round springform
    tin/pan x 6cm/2½in deep –
    bottom and sides buttered and
    lined with parchment or
    greaseproof paper
electric whisk/beater
food processor, blender or nut
    grinder

NOTES

When folding beaten egg whites into a thick batter, first add some of the stiffened whites to the mixture to lighten it, then very gently fold in the remaining whites until just blended – do not overmix or you will crush the egg whites, destroying the volume just beaten into them.

BITTER CHOCOLATE AND ORANGE GANACHE

CONTRIBUTED BY ST QUENTIN RESTAURANT, LONDON

Serves 10 to 12

Equipment
25cm/10in round springform
   tin/pan – buttered and lined
   with parchment or greaseproof
   paper

1 In a heavy-bottomed saucepan, bring the cream to the boil.
2 Remove from the heat and add the chocolate. Stir until the chocolate is dissolved and the mixture is a smooth paste.
3 Add the Grand Marnier (if using) – set the mixture aside.
4 With the peel on, slice the oranges as thinly as possible.
5 In a saucepan over medium heat, dissolve the sugar in the 1 litre/34fl oz (4¼ cups) water.
6 Add the orange slices and simmer for approximately 2 hours, until the oranges are nearly caramelized.
7 Spread a third of the chocolate mixture on the bottom of the tin and cover with half of the orange slices.
8 Top the oranges with half of the remaining chocolate mixture, and cover with the remaining orange slices.
9 Finish with a layer of the remaining chocolate mixture and place in the freezer until firm (several hours or overnight).
10 Slice and serve straight from the freezer, garnished with small dollops of whipped cream topped with julienne strips of candied orange peel.

INGREDIENTS

900ml/30fl oz (3¾ cups)
   double/heavy cream
1 kg/2lb 3oz very good dark plain
   chocolate – broken into small
   pieces
1 Tbl Grand Marnier – optional
6 oranges – washed and dried
1 kg/2lb 3oz caster/superfine sugar
1 litre/34fl oz (4¼ cups) water

To garnish
whipped cream
candied julienne orange peel

NOTES

Chocolat Amer à l'Ecorce
d'Orange (French)

GLACÉ LEMON SPONGE CAKE

CONTRIBUTED BY VALERIE HOBSON, HAMPSHIRE, ENGLAND

INGREDIENTS

120g/4oz (8 Tbl) unsalted butter –
room temperature
175g/6oz caster/superfine sugar
2 large eggs
175g/6oz (1¼ cups) self-raising
flour
grated rind of 1 lemon
4 Tbl fresh lemon juice

For the lemon glacé icing
3 Tbl icing/confectioners' sugar –
sieved
3 Tbl fresh lemon juice

To garnish
icing/confectioners' sugar
whipped cream

1 Preheat the oven to 190°C/375°F/Gas Mark 5.

2 In a bowl, cream the butter and sugar together.

3 Add the eggs one at a time, beating continuously until the mixture is light and fluffy.

4 Fold in the flour, grated rind and lemon juice and beat until smooth (add a few drops of water or more lemon juice, if necessary).

5 Pour the batter into the tin and bake for approximately 40 minutes or until golden brown (a cocktail stick/toothpick inserted into the middle of the cake will come out clean when the cake is done).

6 Meanwhile prepare the icing by mixing together, in a small bowl, the sugar and lemon juice until well combined.

7 Pour the icing over the cake while it is still in the tin and hot from the oven.

8 Let the cake cool in the tin on a rack.

9 Remove the cake from the tin, dust it with sieved icing sugar and serve with generous amounts of whipped cream.

Serves 8 to 10

Equipment
23cm/9in round cake tin/pan –
buttered and lined with
parchment or greaseproof
paper

STICKY DATE CAKE

....

CONTRIBUTED BY DELIA SMITH, SUFFOLK, ENGLAND

INGREDIENTS

....

115g/4oz (¾ cup) raisins
225g/8oz (1¼ cups) chopped
    dates
175g/6oz (1 cup) sultanas
115g/4oz (¾ cup) currants
285g/10oz margarine
2 × 225g/8oz tins (2 cups)
    condensed milk
300ml/10fl oz (1¼ cups) water
150g/5¼oz (1¼ cups) plain/all
    purpose flour
150g/5¼oz (1¼ cups)
    wholemeal/wholewheat flour
¾ tsp bicarbonate of soda/baking
    soda
a pinch of salt
1 rounded Tbl chunky marmalade

1 Arrange a shelf in the middle of the oven and preheat the oven to 170°C/325°F/Gas Mark 3.

2 Place all the fruits, the margarine, condensed milk and water in a saucepan.

3 Bring to the boil, stirring quite frequently to prevent sticking.

4 Let the mixture simmer for exactly 3 minutes, stirring occasionally.

5 Transfer to a large mixing bowl and allow to cool for 30 minutes.

6 Meanwhile, sift the flours, bicarbonate of soda and salt into a large bowl.

7 When the fruit mixture has cooled, stir the flour mixture into it and add the marmalade. Spoon the mixture into the lined tin.

8 Bake for 2½ to 3 hours. Have a look halfway through, and if the top of the cake looks a bit dark put a double square of greaseproof paper on top to protect it.

9 Let the cake cool in the tin for 5 minutes before turning out to cool on a wire tray.

Serves 8 to 10

Equipment
20cm/8in cake tin/pan – lined with parchment or greaseproof paper

NOTES

Adapted from Delia Smith's Book of Cakes, Hodder and Stoughton, 1988.

This large cake keeps for several weeks in an airtight tin and improves with keeping.

Flour is available in many varieties, but unless otherwise specified the term refers to white wheat flour. Flours are graded by the amount of gluten they contain. When a dough is kneaded, its gluten is what helps hold in the gas bubbles generated by the yeast. "Hard" flours have stronger gluten and are therefore best for breads and other yeast pastries. In general British flours are "softer" than American and Canadian varieties.

When you sieve wholemeal flour there is usually some bran left in the sieve: tip it back into the rest of the sieved flour.

FRUIT CAKE

....

CONTRIBUTED BY LADY VERONICA FITZROY, NORFOLK, ENGLAND

Serves 8 to 10

Equipment
20cm/8in square baking tin/pan – lined with foil
pastry brush

1 Preheat the oven to 180°C/350°F/Gas Mark 4.

2 In a large bowl, beat the butter and sugar until creamy.

3 Stir in the eggs.

4 Stir in flour and ground almonds.

5 Add the coated cherries, dried fruits and mixed spice.

6 Pour the batter into the prepared baking tin leaving a well in the middle – since cakes rise towards the centre this helps produce an even surface. Place a piece of greaseproof paper over the top of the batter to prevent burning.

7 Bake for 1 hour, then turn the oven down to 150°C/300°F/Gas Mark 2 and bake for 1 hour more.

8 Test the cake for doneness by inserting a wooden cocktail stick or toothpick into the centre: if it comes out clean, the cake is done.

9 Cool in the baking tin placed on a wire rack.

10 Remove from the tin, carefully turn it upside down and, with a skewer, make numerous holes in the bottom of the cake. Pour the sherry or whisky over the holes, wrap the cake well in foil and store it in an airtight tin.

INGREDIENTS

....

225g/8oz unsalted butter – room temperature

225g/8oz (1 packed cup) dark brown sugar

4 eggs – lightly beaten

225g/8oz (1½ cups) plain/all purpose flour

60g/2oz (½ cup) ground almonds

225g/8oz (2½ cups) glacé cherries – halved, pitted and coated with plain/all purpose flour

680g/1½ lb mixed dried fruits (sultanas, raisins, currants, candied peel, etc)

2 tsp mixed spice

2 Tbl sherry or whisky – or more to taste

NOTES

This is a very good cake for picnic or shooting lunches and can be stored for months if tightly sealed in an airtight tin.

PEACH PIE

....

CONTRIBUTED BY THE ELIZABETH FITZROY HOMES, ENGLAND

INGREDIENTS

900g/2lb fresh peaches – skinned
    and sliced
1 tsp icing/confectioners' sugar

For the crumb crust
225g/8oz digestive biscuits or
    graham crackers
150g/5oz unsalted butter
1 tsp soft light brown sugar
a pinch of cinnamon

To garnish
whipped cream

Preheat the oven to 200°C/400°F/Gas Mark 6.

Prepare the crumb crust:
1 Crush the digestive biscuits into coarse crumbs (use a rolling pin or a food processor).
2 In a large pan, melt the butter and add the brown sugar and cinnamon.
3 Stir in the biscuit crumbs and mix well.
4 Pat the crumb mixture firmly into the buttered pie dish until it evenly coats the bottom and sides.
5 Bake for 7 to 10 minutes or until it starts to brown.
6 Remove from the oven and allow to cool.

Prepare the peaches:
1 Roughly chop 100g/3½oz (1 cup) of the peach slices and place in a saucepan with the icing sugar.
2 Heat the chopped peaches, gently mashing them with a spoon, for 10 minutes.
3 Press through a sieve or purée in a food processor.
4 Return the purée to the saucepan, add the remaining peach slices and simmer gently for 3 minutes.
5 Moisten the pie crust with some of the peach purée.
6 Arrange the peach slices decoratively in the pie shell.
7 Spread remaining purée over the top.
8 Serve chilled, decorated with whipped cream.

Serves 6 to 8

Equipment
23cm/9in pie dish – buttered
sieve or food processor

NOTES

To skin peaches, submerge them very briefly in boiling water then immediately plunge into iced water – the skin will then peel off easily.

Do not warm this pie before serving or the crust will crumble.

BARROOM CHOCOLATE CAKE

CONTRIBUTED BY THE FOUR SEASONS RESTAURANT, NEW YORK CITY

INGREDIENTS

For the chocolate puff pastry
(yields about 1.4kg/3lb of dough,
   enough for 4 cakes)
225g/8oz plain/semi-sweet
   chocolate
450g/1lb unsalted butter – cold
450g/1lb (3 cups) bread flour
180 to 235ml/6 to 8fl oz
   (¾ – 1 cup) cold water

Continued opposite

Prepare the puff pastry dough, at least a day in advance:

1 Place the chocolate in the top of a double boiler over simmering water until melted – let cool to 32°C/90°F.

2 Using a food processor or electric mixer, beat the butter until smooth.

3 Add the melted chocolate and beat until well blended and fairly smooth.

4 Wrap in clingfilm and chill until firm.

5 Place the flour in the work bowl of the food processor or electric mixer.

6 Take a quarter of the chocolate mixture, cut it into small pieces and add it to the flour.

7 Process until the mixture resembles breadcrumbs.

8 With the machine running, add just enough water to bring the dough together to form a ball.

9 On a floured board, knead briefly until smooth. Wrap in greaseproof paper and chill in the refrigerator for 2 hours.

10 Meanwhile, shape the remaining chocolate butter into a 20cm/8in square and keep in a cool place.

11 Place the chilled dough on a floured surface, roll into a 25 x 45cm/10 x 18in rectangle and brush off any excess flour.

12 Leaving a border of about 2.5cm/1in on three sides, place the chocolate butter square over half the dough.

13 Brush the edges of the dough with water and fold the dough in half to enclose the butter.

14 Pressing evenly, roll the dough to a 25 x 45cm/10 x 18in rectangle.

15 Fold the pastry in three (like a business letter).

16 Turn the pastry 90 degrees and repeat steps 14 and 15.

17 Wrap the dough in greaseproof paper or clingfilm and leave to cool in the refrigerator for 15 minutes.

18 Repeat steps 14, 15 and 16.

19 Divide the dough into quarters – wrap each piece well and either refrigerate the dough overnight or freeze for later use.

Serves 10

Equipment
double boiler
food processor or electric mixer
clingfilm/plastic wrap
heavy baking tray/sheet

NOTES

Puff pastry, if tightly wrapped, keeps very well in the freezer and this recipe produces enough pastry for 4 cakes.

Bake the pastry:

1 Roll one piece of the chilled chocolate puff pastry into a 30 x 42cm/12 x 17in rectangle (just over 1mm or ¹⁄₁₆in thick).

2 Place the dough on a heavy, wet baking tray and prick with a fork at 6mm/¼in intervals. Chill for 1 hour.

3 Preheat the oven to 230°C/450°F/Gas Mark 8.

4 Bake the pastry for 25 mins.

5 Let cool to room temperature.

Prepare the chocolate buttercream:

1 Place the egg whites and icing/confectioners' sugar in the top of a double boiler – whisk until heated through and thick (the sugar will completely melt).

2 Transfer the mixture to the bowl of an electric mixer and beat at high speed until it cools to room temperature.

3 In a separate bowl, beat the butter until fluffy and smooth.

4 Add the coffee, chocolate and dark rum to the butter.

5 Beat the egg whites into the butter mixture until smooth.

Assemble and serve:

1 With a serrated knife, cut the pastry crossways into three equal pieces (put the best-looking piece aside for the top).

2 Place one piece of pastry on the work surface and spread with a 1cm/½in layer of buttercream.

3 Top with another piece of pastry and more buttercream.

4 Position the last piece of pastry, flat-side up, and spread with a thin layer of buttercream.

5 Holding the square of chocolate over the cake, make shavings with a vegetable peeler to cover the whole top.

6 Chill the cake until the buttercream is firm.

7 Dip a long serrated knife into very hot water and begin cutting: trim the edges so they are even. Cut the cake in half lengthways. Cut each half crossways into fifths to make 10 equal pieces. Dust each piece with icing sugar, garnish with fresh raspberries and whipped cream if liked, and serve.

INGREDIENTS

For the chocolate buttercream
4 egg whites
175g/6oz (1½ cups)
   icing/confectioners' sugar
225g/8oz unsalted butter –
   softened
2 tsp instant coffee – dissolved in
   2 tsp hot water
115g/4oz plain/semi-sweet
   chocolate – melted and cooled
   to room temperature
2 Tbl dark rum

To garnish
1 square (approximately
   225g/8oz) semi-sweet chocolate
icing/confectioners' sugar
fresh raspberries – optional
whipped cream – optional

BASICS

....

VEGETABLE STOCK

....

Yields 2 litres/3½ pints (8½ cups)
225g/8oz (1½ cups) chopped
    onion
225g/8oz (1¾ cups) chopped
    unpeeled courgette/zucchini
225g/8oz (1¾ cups) chopped
    carrot
225g/8oz (1¾ cups) chopped
    celery
140g/5oz (1¼ cups) chopped
    fennel
3 cloves garlic – chopped
1 coriander root (or 1 tsp
    coriander seeds)
1 star anise
10 peppercorns
6 sprigs fresh parsley
2 bay leaves
2 sprigs tarragon
2 litres/3½ pints (8½ cups) cold
    water
3 slices lemon

1 Place all the ingredients,
except the lemon, in a stock
pot, and cover them with the
cold water. Bring to the boil.
2 Lower the heat and
simmer for 20 minutes.
3 Add the lemon slices.
Cover the pan, turn off the
heat and allow to cool.
4 Let sit for a minimum of 4
hours, or refrigerate
overnight.

5 Strain and pass through a
fine sieve.
Adjust vegetables and herbs
to suit preference and availability. The addition of any
leftover raw vegetables
(asparagus or broccoli stems,
green beans, potatoes –
almost anything except beetroot) would only make the
stock more interesting.

FISH STOCK

....

Yields 2 litres/3½ pints (8½ cups)
900g/2lb fish bones and heads
    (from non-oily fish)
30g/1oz (2 Tbl) unsalted butter
200g/7oz (1¾ cups) chopped
    white part of leek
200g/7oz (1¼ cups) chopped
    onion
100g/3½oz (¾ cup) sliced carrot
100g/3½oz (¾ cup) chopped
    celery
100g/3½oz (¾ cup) chopped
    fennel
150ml/5fl oz (½ cup + 2 Tbl)
    dry white wine
2.5 litres/4¼ pints (10½ cups)
    cold water
2 slices lemon
1 coriander root (or 1 tsp
    coriander seeds)
4 sprigs fresh parsley
2 bay leaves
2 sprigs fresh thyme
12 white peppercorns

1 Rinse the fish, removing
any gills, and roughly chop
them.
2 In a stock pot, melt the
butter. Add the leek and
onion and sauté until tender.
3 Add the fish and the
remaining vegetables. Sweat
over a low heat for 5
minutes, stirring.
4 Pour in the wine, increase
the heat and cook until it has
almost evaporated.
5 Cover with the cold water,
bring to a rapid boil and
skim off any foam that rises
to the surface.
6 Add the lemon, herbs and
peppercorns, lower the heat
and simmer, uncovered, for
no more than 20 minutes.
(If fish bones are simmered
for longer than 20 minutes
the stock may turn bitter.
If the bones are removed,
however, the stock can be
further reduced without
damaging its flavour.)
7 Strain the stock then pass it
through a muslin-lined sieve
– reserve.

CHICKEN STOCK

....

Yields 2 litres/3½ pints (8½ cups)
60g/2oz (4 Tbl) unsalted butter
900g/2lb uncooked chicken,
    preferably wings, carcasses

or a whole stewing fowl –
    roughly chopped
200g/7oz (1¾ cups) chopped
    white part of leek
200g/7oz (1¼ cups) chopped
    onion
140g/5oz (1¼ cups) chopped
    celery
140g/5oz (1¼ cups) chopped
    carrot
2 cloves garlic – roughly
    chopped
150ml/5fl oz (½ cup + 2 Tbl)
    dry white wine
3 litres/5 pints (12½ cups) cold
    water
5 sprigs fresh parsley
10 peppercorns
2 bay leaves
3 sprigs fresh thyme
2 cloves

1 In a stock pot, melt the
butter. Add the chicken and
stir until lightly coloured.
2 Add the leek, onion,
celery, carrot and garlic and
continue cooking for 5 more
minutes, stirring occasionally.
3 Add the wine and cook
until the alcohol has
evaporated (approximately
3 minutes).
4 Cover with the cold water
and bring rapidly to the boil.
Boil vigorously for
5 minutes, skimming foam
that rises to the surface.

5 Add the herbs and spices, lower the heat and simmer gently, partially covered, for 2 to 3 hours, skimming when necessary.
6 Strain and allow to cool, uncovered.
7 Cover and refrigerate overnight.
8 Scrape off any congealed fat from the surface of the stock.

BROWN VEAL, BEEF OR LAMB STOCK

Yields 2 litres/3½ pints (8½ cups)
150ml/5fl oz (½ cup + 2 Tbl) vegetable oil
900g/2lb veal, beef or lamb bones and trimmings (preferably fatty ones)
400g/14oz (2½ cups) chopped onions
200g/7oz (1½ cups) chopped carrots
100g/3½oz (¾ cup) chopped celery with leaves
100g/3½oz (1 cup) wiped and chopped mushrooms (preferably field)
450g/1lb fresh tomatoes – roughly chopped (or 225g/8oz chopped tinned tomatoes in purée)
90ml/3fl oz (6 Tbl) tarragon vinegar for veal stock or 180ml/6fl oz (¾ cup) dry red wine for beef or lamb stock

3 litres/5 pints (12½ cups) cold water
5 cloves garlic – halved
herbs: 6 × 8cm/3in sprigs fresh thyme, 8 sprigs fresh parsley, 2 bay leaves
spices: 6 peppercorns, plus for lamb stock 4 juniper berries, for beef stock 4 whole cloves

1 In a large roasting tin, heat 90ml/3fl oz (6 Tbl) of the oil. Add the bones and trimmings, stir to coat with the oil, then lower the heat and brown slowly.
2 Meanwhile, in a stock pot heat the remaining 60ml/2fl oz (4 Tbl) oil, add the onions, carrots, celery and mushrooms and brown them. Stir frequently and be careful not to burn the vegetables.
3 When the bones are thoroughly caramelized, drain off excess oil. Add the tomatoes and vinegar or wine to the roasting tin and gently scrape to incorporate caramelized cooking juices.
4 Add the meat mixture to the vegetables and cover with the cold water. Cover the pot and bring to the boil over high heat.
5 Boil rapidly for 5 minutes, skimming any foam that comes to the surface.
6 Add the garlic, herbs and spices, lower the heat and

simmer gently, partially covered, for 4 hours, skimming when necessary.
7 Strain the stock then pass it through a muslin-lined sieve. Either use/store the stock as it is or return it to a clean pan and reduce further to make glaze/essence or thickened stock.

THICKENED STOCK (FOND DE … LIÉ)

Yields 120ml/4fl oz (½ cup)
600ml/1 pint (2½ cups) hot stock
1 tsp cornflour/cornstarch or arrowroot
2 tsp cold stock
salt and freshly ground pepper to taste

1 Over medium heat, reduce the stock by three-quarters to 150ml/5fl oz (10 Tbl).
2 In a small bowl, blend the cornflour or arrowroot into the cold stock until smooth. Whisk this into the reduced stock and simmer for 20 minutes.
3 Strain through a fine sieve, season and keep warm.

WHEN MAKING STOCK:

Do not add salt – salt will be added to the final sauce or dish and you don't want to salt it twice.

Use cold water – this helps to solidify impurities, forcing them to come to the surface of the stock where they will be skimmed off.

Simmer stocks, do not boil them, or the force of the boil will trap impurities and make the stock cloudy.

Be careful not to allow any ingredients to burn during initial browning. If you later incorporate burned bits into the stock it will be bitter. If the stock catches on the bottom of the pot, transfer immediately to a clean pot and continue cooking.

If time permits, allow stock to cool uncovered and refrigerate overnight. The fat will rise to the top and congeal, where it can be easily scraped off.

Stock keeps in the refrigerator for only 2 to 3 days, but it freezes very well. Reduce the stock before freezing it if space in the freezer storage capacity is tight; the stock can be diluted later. Stock may be frozen in ice-cube trays, then stored in plastic bags in the freezer. Each cube will be roughly 1 Tbl.

BIOGRAPHIES OF CONTRIBUTORS

AL FORNO
*Chefs: Johanne Killeen and
George Germon*
Al Forno's co-chefs, Johanne
Killeen and George Germon,
have won numerous US awards
for the down-to-earth style of
their version of absolutely
heavenly trattoria cooking. This
hearty fare is set out in an
atmosphere of exposed beams,
open fires and romantic table
settings. The combination of
fresh ingredients meticulously
prepared, and a cosy environ-
ment, makes it very difficult for
Al Forno's patrons to stay away.
577 South Main Street,
Providence, Rhode Island, USA
Tel: (401) 273 9760

ANNABEL'S
Mark Birley's nightclub in
Berkeley Square, Annabel's, has
been a favourite haunt of
sophisticated internationals
since the sixties. The atmosphere is "country-house chic".
Walls hung with oil paintings
and banquettes comfortably
cushioned in the finest English
materials combine with its
excellent food and impeccable
service to make this private
club one of the best in the
world.
44 Berkeley Square,
London
Tel: (0171) 429 3558

LORD ARCHER
Here is a multi-talented gentle-
man who has somehow found
the time to be creative in the

kitchen. He is well known for
his political career (launched at
the age of 26) and, of course,
for his blockbuster novels.
Happily for the Elizabeth
FitzRoy Homes, Jeffrey Archer's
personal involvement in
charitable works throughout
Great Britain has enabled us to
sample his culinary talents.

THE ARMY AND NAVY CLUB
Founded in 1837, the Army
and Navy Club may not be the
most famous club in London
but it has frequently been
acclaimed as the best. Over the
years its members have come
to depend on the home-style
cooking steeped in tradition
and executed with flair. Head
chef Satish Desigar demonstrates this daily. His experi-
ences in India and in numerous
top positions on the continent
have allowed him successfully
to meld eastern with western
cuisine.
Pall Mall, London
Tel: (0171) 930 9721

JANE ASHER
Jane Asher's acting career is
serious, and based on talent
and intelligence, not just a
beautiful face. In recent times,
we have seen another side to
her accomplishments. Jane
makes and decorates cakes in a
witty and imaginative way.
What started as a hobby is
now a substantial business in
Chelsea, London, and Jane's
cakes are also available from
Sainsbury's supermarkets for
every family in Britain to enjoy.

AZIZA'S
Near Peranakan Place,
Singapore, Aziza's is the name-
sake restaurant of Aziza Ali –
Malaysian food's most celebrated champion. Ms Ali's personal
charm and boundless enthusi-
asm for Malaysian cuisine and
culture have made her restaurant a required stop for any
visitor to Singapore. She is
always eager to introduce
others to the cuisine of which
she is so justifiably proud.
36 Emerald Hill Road,
Singapore
Tel: 235 1130

BALLYMALOE HOUSE
On a 400-acre farm on the
south coast of Ireland, only two
miles from the sea, is
Ballymaloe Country House
Hotel, established in 1964 by
Ivan and Myrtle Allen. Fresh
produce from Ballymaloe's farm
and vast quantities of fresh
seafood are a mainstay in this
beautifully appointed, grand
farmhouse.
Shanagarry, Midleton,
County Cork, Ireland
Tel: (021) 652 531

BLAKES HOTEL
Chef: Neville Campbell
Perhaps the most successful
and certainly the most exotical-
ly decorated of the London
townhouse hotels, Blakes offers
its clients a feast of styles,
bringing together classic
simplicity and the opulence of
the French Empire (they have
Josephine's day bed.). The
emphasis is on comfort and

intimacy. In the elegantly
contemporary (and glamorous)
restaurant, Neville Campbell is
famous for his adaptation of Far
East recipes, resulting in dishes
that are captivatingly original.
33 Roland Gardens,
London
Tel: (0171) 370 6701

BODYSGALLEN HALL
Steeped in history and
surrounded by the dramatically
beautiful Welsh countryside,
Bodysgallen Hall is a
remarkable example of period
restoration. The house is luxuriously comfortable without
having sacrificed any of its
beautiful period detail, and the
gardens have many rare, classic
features. The hotel's delightful
restaurant uses an imaginative
mixture of the best of English
and Welsh cuisine.
Llandudno,
Gwynedd, Wales
Tel: (01492) 584 466

BOODLE'S
This smart social and non-polit-
ical club was founded in 1762
by William Almack and named
after its first manager. It soon
acquired a reputation for good
gambling, good food and excellent sociability. Beau Brummell
and the Duke of Wellington
belonged to the club. In 1897,
the members bought Boodle's
and moved it to its present
elegant location.
28 St James's Street,
London
Tel: (0171) 930 7166

THE BOULDERS
Chef: Charles Wiley
This is one of the world's most prestigious luxury resorts, nestled in the spectacular Sonoran Desert sixteen miles northeast of Phoenix. This very special, imaginatively designed hideaway blends seamlessly into the surrounding desert terrain. Guests enjoy world-class golf, tennis and fitness facilities, spacious adobe casitas with wood-burning fireplaces and private terraces, and spectacular southwestern and Grand American cuisine. The award-winning chef, Charles Wiley, was recently named one of the top ten "Best Chefs in the US" by *Food and Wine* magazine.
Box 2090, Carefree,
Arizona, USA
Tel: (602) 488 9009

ED BRADLEY
US television journalist Ed Bradley is a long-time regular on CBS's flagship current affairs programme, *60 Minutes*. He was introduced to cooking as a boy while helping out in his father's Detroit restaurant. When his globe-trotting schedule permits, he enjoys casual evenings of cooking and conversation with friends in his specially designed open kitchen. Mr Bradley has generously contributed one of his super-spicy house specialities along with a piece of advice: "Keep plenty of water available!"

MRS BARBARA BUSH
During her husband's presidency, Barbara Bush brought a dignity and serenity to the job of being First Lady. She won respect and affection from both sides of the political divide and was a great asset to President Bush on the international stage. Her work for medical and children's charities and especially her efforts to promote literacy have confirmed her reputation as a woman whose public life has not eclipsed her private concern for people.

THE CAPITAL HOTEL
Small, perpetually fashionable and quiet, this twenty-year-old hotel located in Knightsbridge is as well known for its excellent restaurant as it is for its comfortable rooms. The Capital is "a place for serious eating". Its sophisticated menu attracts locals appreciative of fine cuisine as well as visitors who have heard of its superb Anglo-French food.
22–24 Basil Street,
London
Tel: (0171) 589 5171

THE CARLTON CLUB
This is the only politically affiliated gentlemen's club in London. One must be a member of the Conservative Party to be considered for club membership. Chef Irwin prides himself on his very traditional cooking as well as his ability to select and train Master Chefs of the future.
69 St James's Street,
London
Tel: (0171) 493 1164

CHESERY GSTAAD
Chef: Robert Speth
Robert Speth trained as a confectioner and chef at the famous Restaurant Waldhorn, Ravensburg, in his native Germany. From there he spent time in Cap d'Antibes and the Restaurant Oasis in La Napule. Since 1984, he has lived in Gstaad, working at the Restaurant Chesery. This magnificent chalet was built by Prince Sadruddin Aga Khan. Chef Speth leased the Inn in 1989 and now runs it himself.
Gstaad, Switzerland
Tel: (030) 42 451

CHEZ NICO AT NINETY
Nico Ladenis looks close to achieving legendary status in the London restaurant world. His move into the Grosvenor House on Park Lane has been a huge success – reserving a table is still the gastronomic equivalent of getting stalls tickets for the opera at Covent Garden. Nico's artistry, like that of an opera singer, continues to develop, with a recent return to the classic repertoire always enlivened by invention and experiment.
90 Park Lane, London
Tel: (0171) 409 1290

CHIANG MAI RESTAURANT
Chef: Vatcharin Bhumichitr
The Chiang Mai, owned by Chef Bhumichitr, is probably the most famous proponent of Thai cuisine outside Bangkok. It is the first and only restaurant in the west to present high quality Thai regional cooking and it has also introduced London to the exciting Thai vegetarian tradition. Chef Bhumichitr has contributed his personal recipe for the most popular of all Thai dishes, and one which has acquainted many foreigners with the complex mix of flavours and textures which characterize this cuisine.
48 Frith Street, London
Tel: (0171) 437 7444

ARRIGO CIPRIANI
Arrigo Cipriani's famous Venice establishment, Harry's Bar, is located on the banks of the romantic Grand Canal just steps from St Mark's Square. The colourful downstairs bar area offers satisfying casual dishes and exceptional beverages, including the legendary "Bellini" (freshly squeezed white peach juice and sparkling Italian white wine), while the serene upstairs dining room has a more elegant ambience.
Calle Vallaresso 1323,
Venice, Italy
Tel: 528 5777

HOTEL CIPRIANI
Set on its own three-acre island in a beautiful lagoon, the Cipriani provides a peaceful contrast to the bustle of Venice itself. Relaxed but unfailingly elegant, the hotel restaurant's service and cuisine remain historically flawless.
Giudecca 10, Venice, Italy
Tel: (041) 520 7744

CITRUS
Chef: Michel Richard
This chic, white, airy restaurant with glass-brick walls draws a fashionable crowd each lunch- and dinner-time. They come not just for the setting, though the paintings and the flowers on the leafy patio are delightful, but to enjoy the food of one of the most exuberant, creative French chefs in the United States today. In his Los Angeles restaurant, Chef Richard has conjured up a cuisine that is classically French and yet casual in the best Californian tradition.
6703 Melrose Avenue, Los Angeles, California, USA
Tel: (213) 857 0034

CLARIDGE'S
Chef: Marjan Lesnik
One of the most prestigious and elegant hotels in London, in operation since 1812, this restaurant with its Art Deco design boasts the finest French and British cuisine and well-chosen wines. Claridge's remains a very popular West End rendezvous for pre- and after-theatre suppers in the Causerie. Chef Lesnik, Maître Chef des Cuisines, has seen his lamb entrée become a signature dish.
Brook Street, London
Tel: (0171) 629 8860

CLARKE'S
Chef/proprietor: Sally Clarke
English-born Sally Clarke's training and experience has ranged from Paris to California. With that unique and eclectic mix she has made her own restaurant a London landmark and has helped to introduce new influences to English culinary traditions.
124 Kensington Church Street, London
Tel: (0171) 221 9225

THE COMPLEAT KITCHEN
Trained in South Africa and with a background in corporate home economics, Judy Marjoribanks has been running this upmarket cookshop for six years. She has developed the business to include a studio where she teaches a range of cookery courses. Enthusiastic amateurs come into the friendly school to brush up on summer desserts, cake-making or winter dinner-party food – or to get right back to basics on Judy's foundation course.
9 The Woolmarket, Cirencester, Gloucestershire, England
Tel: (01285) 652240

LISA DAVIDSON
Lisa Davidson is a former television newsreader with the BBC World Television News Service. She is the author of several biographies. Ms Davidson lives in Oxfordshire, England, with her husband, two small children and three step-children. Without any formal training to which to attribute her good sense of cooking, she cites the influences of Delia Smith, her mother, and necessity.

JOSCELINE DIMBLEBY
Josceline Dimbleby has long been regarded as one of Britain's brightest and most innovative cookery writers. Her regular column in the *Sunday Telegraph* is prescribed reading for food-lovers, and the books she has produced for Sainsbury's supermarkets since 1976 have given a generation of cooks courage and inspiration in the kitchen.

THE DINING ROOM AT THE RITZ-CARLTON BUCKHEAD
Chef: Guenter Seeger
German-born Chef Seeger recognized his passion for cooking as a young boy, growing up in his parents' wholesale fruit and vegetable business. The restaurant he kept as a young man, near the Black Forest, was one of the first outside France to be awarded a Michelin star. Now in charge of the Dining Room, he inspires local farmers to grow their best and sometimes their most unusual produce for his kitchen where he cooks an eclectic mix of European and American food.
3434 Peachtree Road NE, Atlanta, Georgia, USA
Tel: (404) 237 2700

DOMINICK DUNNE
American-born author, journalist and contributing editor to *Vanity Fair* magazine, Dominick Dunne has recently discovered a new talent: cooking. As Mr Dunne pointed out, his spinach dip demonstrates how quickly and deliciously one can put together a canapé as the guests come up the drive.

VICTOR EDELSTEIN
In the world of fashion Victor Edelstein has long been a name to revere. A couturier in the grand tradition, he has been responsible for many of the

Princess of Wales's glamorous and much photographed evening outfits. When not busy creating in cloth, Mr Edelstein's pleasure is entertaining at home, and his reputation is of a charming and generous host.

ELIZABETH ON 37TH
Chef/owner: Elizabeth B. Terry
Situated in a lovingly restored "Grande Home" on a charming tree-shaded street, this gourmet restaurant is famous for its gracious service and satisfying New Southern cuisine. Awarded the coveted DiRoNa (Distinguished Restaurants of North America) in 1993, it was also named as "One of the Top 25 Restaurants in America" by *Food and Wine* magazine. Celebrated chef/owner Elizabeth Terry's inspired approach to classic dishes employs light, health-conscious techniques, yet maximizes the deep flavour combinations that have made American southern cuisine so famous.
105 East 37th Street, Savannah, Georgia, USA
Tel: (912) 236 5547

FLEUR DE LYS
Chef/owner: Hubert Keller
A sumptuously decorated 80-seat restaurant near the Union Square section of San Francisco, this is one of the most exciting gourmet destinations in the United States. Hubert Keller, a world-travelled native of Alsace, offers his guests dishes that feature glorious Californian ingredients imaginatively spiked with exotic seasonings and presented with all the finesse associated with the best French tradition.
777 Sutter Street, San Francisco, California, USA
Tel: (415) 673 7779

THE FOUR SEASONS RESTAURANT

With its combination of seasonal menus, classical culinary technique, striking ambience and legendary personal service, the Four Seasons Restaurant has been at the pinnacle of Manhattan dining for generations. By simply guaranteeing its patrons "the very best", this beautiful restaurant has come to enjoy a loyal clientele and a reputation for excellence.
99 East 52nd Street,
New York City
Tel: (212) 754 9494

GADDI'S, AT THE PENINSULA HOTEL

The Peninsula Hotel in Kowloon, the most famous hotel in Hong Kong, is known to generations of travellers as "the Pen". Tea in the gilded lobby has been an institution since the hotel was built in 1928. The Pen has just re-emerged after a major renovation, boasting 300 guest rooms with spectacular views of Hong Kong, each room equipped with the latest in telecommunications. Gaddi's, the most distinguished restaurant in Hong Kong, is an integral part of the Peninsula's reputation, upholding its tradition of excellence for international cuisine.
Salisbury Road, Tsimshatsui,
Hong Kong
Tel: 2366 6251

PRINCESS GALITZINE

When Prince and Princess George Galitzine helped Mark Birley organize a Russian fortnight at Annabel's in the 1960s, Princess Galitzine produced this recipe for kissel there ever since. The princess is now involved with a library that she and her daughter Katya founded in

Russia in memory of Prince George, situated in his mother's house at 46 Fontanka, St Petersburg. When they have a special gathering there, kissel is sure to be on the menu.

LE GAVROCHE

In Britain, the Roux name has become synonymous with excellence. Le Gavroche, the restaurant opened by Albert and his brother Michel in 1967, was the first in this country to be distinguished with three Michelin rosettes. Their widespread interests include shops, contract catering and, of course, successful restaurants – all of which guarantee that the Roux influence will be long-lived.
43 Upper Brook Street,
London
Tel: (0171) 408 0881

LA GAZELLE D'OR

This Moroccan oasis is one of the world's most romantic destinations. A small resort of thirty cottage-style rooms, it is set in twenty acres of fragrant tropical gardens and gently bubbling fountains. Guests relax amid beautiful antiques, Berber carpets, handmade furniture and fantastic tented ceilings. By riding horses across the desert, playing tennis, or swimming in the beautiful garden pool, guests can work up an appetite for the restaurant's world-class Moroccan/French cuisine.
Taroudant, Morocco
Tel: (8) 85 20 48

GIDLEIGH PARK

Chef: Shaun Hill
Set on the edge of spectacular Dartmoor, this handsome, comfortable hotel has developed a wide reputation for the high standards of its hospitality. Chef Shaun Hill's imaginative cuisine, overseen by

co-proprietor Kay Henderson, successfully combines influences from the Far East, provincial France and Tuscany.
Chagford, Devon, England
Tel: (01647) 432367

GIRARDET

Chef: Frédy Girardet
The Girardet Restaurant in Lausanne is considered by many to be one of the finest restaurants in the world. Frédy Girardet has a reputation as a brilliant innovator, uncompromising in his use of the highest quality ingredients and in his quest for perfection.
1 Rue d'Yverdon, Crissier,
Lausanne, Switzerland
Tel: (021) 634 05 05

HAMBLETON HALL

This elegant and imposing Victorian House is situated a hundred miles north of London in a spectacular lakeside setting. The restaurant is particularly well known for fine food and wine with exceptional game specialities in the winter.
A well-stocked kitchen garden and excellent supplies of fresh fish inspire the summer menu.
Hambleton, near Oakham,
Leicestershire, England
Tel: (01572) 756991

HARRY'S BAR, LONDON

Owned by Mark Birley, in partnership with James Sherwood, Harry's Bar is a private dining club in Mayfair. Modelled on Harry's Bar in Venice, this beautifully appointed club with its attentive waiters and superb Italian cuisine provides an unrivalled experience.
26 South Audley Street,
London
Tel: (0171) 408 0844

HOTEL HASSLER

For generations one of Rome's most prestigious addresses, this refined 100-room bastion of luxury boasts a spectacular location atop the Spanish Steps, temptingly close to Rome's chic shopping promenades. Renowned for elegant service and attention to detail, the dramatic rooftop restaurant offers unrivalled views of the Eternal City along with memorable Italian cuisine. The Hassler's unique blend of discreet Old World elegance and state-of-the-art amenities sets this grand hotel apart from the competition.
Piazza Trinita dei Monti 6,
Rome, Italy
Tel: 678 2651

MARIE HELVIN

Here is a celebrity who has a delightfully cosmopolitan attitude to food. Hawaiian-born Marie has a Japanese mother and a Danish-American father. She came to Europe as a model, became Mrs David Bailey and for a decade reigned as the most photographed beauty in Britain. She is enjoying new challenges now, presenting her first exercise video *Body and Soul* and seeing publication of her second book, *Body Pure*.

HEMINGWAY'S RESTAURANT

Chef/owner: Ted Fondulas
This is an acclaimed gourmet enclave nestling at the foot of Vermont's popular Killington Mountain ski area. Named one of the "Top 25 Restaurants in the United States" by *Food and Wine* magazine, Hemingway's Restaurant is in a restored 1860s farmhouse, imaginatively

decorated with colourful modern art. Chef Fondulas presents a classically inspired, changing menu of flavourful seasonal dishes which show off local produce and specialities to their best advantage.
Route 4, Killington,
Vermont, USA
Tel: (802) 422 3886

VALERIE HOBSON

Valerie Hobson was only fifteen when she first appeared on the stage at Drury Lane, London. Though trained as a ballet dancer, she was soon snapped up by Hollywood and had great fun making mystery and horror movies for a couple of years. She returned to England and a major career as an actress when the British film industry was at its peak. Valerie paints, writes and enjoys the pleasures of books and music between work on one of her several charitable committees. She is married to Mr John Profumo.

THE HUNGRY MONK

Since 1968 Nigel and Sue MacKenzie have devoted themselves to this small, charming country restaurant. The open fires and low beamed ceilings provide the perfect setting for their inventive but accessible English food based on French principles. As in France, there is a terrific emphasis here on the freshness of the ingredients. They have borrowed the concept of the fixed-price menu too, which is becoming a welcome trend in British restaurants.
The Street, Jevington, near Polegate, East Sussex, England
Tel: (01323) 482178

L'INCONTRO

Gino Santin, who owns this restaurant as well as another in London and one in Milan, is author of *La Cucina Veneziana*. In this smart and incontestably chic establishment, he presents Venetian specialities – home-made pastas, salt cod, baked scallops, beef with truffles – to a discerning audience. Gino's philosophy is that good food is beautiful in itself, but if you can eat it in a stylish, modern restaurant so much the better.
87 Pimlico Road, London
Tel: (0171) 730 6327

JASPER'S

Tell a Bostonian that you would like to take him or her for a splendid dinner in town and this is the restaurant where you will be making a reservation. In the spacious but muted dining rooms, Jasper White presents his culinary wizardry, re-inventing dishes from around the world and presenting the best *nouvelle* New England *cuisine*.
240 Commercial Street,
Boston, Massachusetts, USA
Tel: (617) 523 1126

JOE'S

This modern, split-level brasserie decorated with ecru wall panelling, natural leather seating and warm white tones is unashamedly urban. Both clientele and staff are cosmopolitan and the place rings with busy conversation. The menu is broadminded, reflecting modern British cuisine with a Mediterranean twist.
126 Draycott Avenue,
London
Tel: (0171) 225 2217

KEN LO'S MEMORIES OF CHINA RESTAURANT

Chinese born, Kenneth H.C. Lo is a Cambridge graduate and author of some thirty-seven cookery books. His Memories of China restaurants have put oriental cooking on the gourmet map, and his BBC series filmed on location in China has brought this cuisine to a wide audience. The restaurant demonstrates Mr Lo's talents in the artistry of blending colour, texture and shape, so important in the Orient.
Chelsea Harbour, Lots Road, London
Tel: (0171) 352 4953

KINLOCH LODGE HOTEL

Lord and Lady MacDonald own this comfortable seventeenth-century hotel on the Isle of Skye. You will find it at the end of a long drive in a secluded spot with wonderful views across Loch na Dal to the rugged mainland hills beyond. Tranquillity prevails throughout the house. Guests enjoy country sports or just retreat from the world. The dining room, hung with family portraits, is the setting for Lady MacDonald's excellent cooking, which relies heavily on good local produce, especially seafood.
Sleat, Isle of Skye, Highland, Scotland
Tel: (0147 13) 214

MRS GLENYS KINNOCK

A very attractive personality in her own right, as well as always having been a great asset to the career of her husband the former Labour leader Neil Kinnock, Glenys Kinnock earned popularity as a woman who could manage the limelight yet retain her

down-to-earth common sense. It is because of these qualities that she has gone on to become a radio broadcaster and a Member of the European Parliament for South Wales East. It is common knowledge among family and friends that she is a very good cook. How she finds time to produce such mouth-watering dishes is truly a tribute to her many skills.

LEITH'S

Prue Leith has become something of a legend on the British food scene since she first started her small outside catering business in 1962. She now employs a staff of 350 and has annual sales in excess of £7 million. Leith's restaurant has always been the most well-known public face of the business, a wonderfully seductive restaurant that retains the atmosphere of a private house. The food is well cooked and intelligently put together from superb ingredients at a reasonable price.
92 Kensington Park Road, London
Tel: (0171) 229 4481

LEITH'S SCHOOL OF FOOD AND WINE

Founded in 1975, Leith's School offers flexible daytime, evening and weekend courses in wine selection and restaurant management as well as in a variety of cuisines. The courses are suitable for the professional and the keen amateur cook. Anyone with ambitions to pursue a career in the catering industry or just to become a more confident cook would find the courses invaluable. The school is run by Caroline Waldegrave and Fiona Burrell.
21 St Albans Grove,
London
Tel: (0171) 229 0177

LUCAS CARTON
Chef: Alain Senderens
Not simply a restaurant, Lucas Carton is a temple to French gastronomy and an historical monument. It is decorated in flamboyant Art Nouveau style – the dining room is beautifully mirrored and even the dining chairs appear in books celebrating French furniture. To eat at the table of the man who has become the philosopher as well as one of the best practitioners of French food is to enjoy an unforgettable experience.
9, Place de la Madeleine, Paris, France
Tel: 42 66 27 37

MRS NORMA MAJOR
Though there are always extraordinary demands being made on Mrs Major, she has managed to retain a serene home life and to continue to pursue her vast cultural interests while also supporting her husband as the British prime minister. Maintaining these responsibilities has not interfered with her knowledge and appreciation of the importance of good food and proper diet.

MALLORY COURT HOTEL
Chef/proprietor: Allan Holland
One of the first English country-house hotels, Mallory Court continues to be one of the best. Built in 1910 in the Elizabethan style with tall chimneys and stone-mullioned windows, the house stands in ten acres of beautifully landscaped garden. In the panelled restaurant Allan Holland offers a satisfying mix of classic and modern styles. It is the perfect weekend retreat.

Harbury Lane, Bishop's Tachbrook, Leamington Spa, Warwickshire, England
Tel: (01926) 330214

THE MANILA HOTEL
Hotels are not generally considered tourist attractions, but the Manila Hotel, besides being one of the loveliest in Asia, is rich in history. General Douglas MacArthur made his home in the penthouse between 1935 and 1941 and vowed to return to the Philippines after the war. Built in 1912, the hotel has an old world mahogany-and-marble opulence and a staff who are proud to provide the best old-fashioned service. Rooms at the hotel overlook the walled city of Intramuros, the most historic part of the city, or Manila Bay, with its fabled sunsets.
1 Rizal Park, Manila, Philippines
Tel: 247 0011

LE MANOIR AUX QUAT' SAISONS
The French nobleman who built this house in the fifteenth century must have looked down with great delight as he watched Raymond Blanc turn it into one of the best hotels and restaurants in the country. From the three-acre kitchen garden where vegetables and herbs are grown, to the wonderful array of fresh fruit that guests find in their rooms, Le Manoir is about the search for perfection. Michael Priest has designed and furnished the dining rooms, the conservatory and the luxurious bedrooms in exquisite yet restrained style.
Church Road, Great Milton, Oxfordshire, England
Tel: (01844) 278881

THE MANSION ON TURTLE CREEK
This is a prestigious 140-room luxury hotel located in a restored 1920s Italian Renaissance-style residential estate five minutes from the central Dallas business district. The opulent restaurant is a showcase for gourmet southwestern cuisine. Author of cookery books on southwestern cuisine and the blend of Asia and the Americas, Dean Fearing is a bold chef whose combinations of vibrant flavour, colour and texture have earned him celebrity status.
2821 Turtle Creek Boulevard, Dallas, Texas, USA
Tel: (214) 559 2100

MARK'S CLUB
In the heart of Mayfair is Mark's Club, one of Mark Birley's three private dining clubs. Decorated with luxurious fabrics and large Victorian paintings, it has a comfortable, discreet and sophisticated atmosphere, reminiscent of an English country house. The dining room is quiet and elegant, the service impeccable and the food consistently excellent.
46 Charles Street, London
Tel: (0171) 499 1360

MERIDIEN BAAN BORAN
Deep within Southeast Asia's dramatically beautiful Golden Triangle on the plains of the Mekong river, the Meridien Baan Boran is an excellent base for exploring Thailand's northern interior by longtail boat or even by elephant. The hotel is built in traditional style and brings together eastern cuisine and hospitality and the highest international standards of comfort and amenity.
Chiang Saen, Chaing Rai, Thailand
Tel: (053) 716678

MOREL'S
Chef/proprietor: Jean-Yves Morel
Jean-Yves Morel holds a coveted Michelin Rose for his excellent and faultlessly presented food in Haslemere, where the headquarters of the Elizabeth FitzRoy Homes is also situated. The food is classic French and the menu encouragingly short. The dining room is summery blue and cream, the service attentive and highly professional. Students of the restaurant business could learn a lot by camping out on the doorstep of Morel's.
23 Lower Street, Haslemere, Surrey, England
Tel: (01428) 651462

MOSIMANN'S
Swiss-born Anton Mosimann is renowned for his culinary career, having worked throughout Europe, Canada, the Far East and Japan. In 1985, he created *cuisine naturelle*, a method of healthy cooking which eschews the use of fats and alcohol. He has written several cookery books, been the subject of two television series; and, in 1988, he opened his private dining club, Mosimann's. He recently masterminded the Duke of Edinburgh's seventieth birthday celebrations – a party for 1400 in the grounds of Windsor Castle.
11 West Halkin Street, London
Tel: (0171) 235 9625

MOTCOMBS
This popular establishment tucked underneath an equally fashionable wine bar attracts a smart local crowd. Charmingly decorated with oil paintings and offering up unpretentious

but delicious English food, owner Philip Lawless has discovered the formula for a successful Belgravia restaurant and created a loyal clientele.
26 Motcomb Street,
London
Tel: (0171) 235 6382

THE OLD RECTORY
The torch for fine cooking on the North Wales coast is kept burning by Wendy Vaughan of the Old Rectory. Wendy always had ambitions to become a chef but was discouraged at school. She became a nurse for a brief period but her culinary ambitions resurfaced when she and her husband bought the Rectory and turned it into a small hotel. From the canapés and homemade breads through excellent seafood and lightly cooked vegetables to delicious puddings and petit fours, Wendy's table is perfection. Residents may dine together at the long dining table or separately, the choice is theirs. Wendy has won the *Good Food Guide's* award for Best Country Restaurant in the region and is a Michelin Red M Chef.
Llansanffraid Glan Conwy,
near Conwy, Gwynedd, Wales
Tel: (01492) 580611

HOTEL OKURA
This hotel enjoys a reputation as one of the most distinguished in the world, due in no small measure to its legendary efficiency and superb management. Stylish attention to detail and personalized service have made the Hotel Okura the favourite Tokyo address for visiting royalty, politicians and business people.
2-10-4 Toranomon, Minato-Ku, Tokyo, Japan
Tel: (03) 3582 0111

THE PEAT INN
The Auld Alliance between Scotland and France has found an echo in David and Patricia Wilson's Peat Inn, a former coaching inn. The raw materials are the best in Scotland — venison, beef, lobster and spring lamb, served in a dining room that has the elegant period formality of a French country restaurant. Guests wax lyrical about the seven-course tasting menu, and a lucky few stay at the Inn in one of eight luxury suites.
Cupar, Fife, Scotland
Tel: (01334) 840206

LES PRÉS D'EUGÉNIE
This is the perfect French country inn, where Michel and Christine Guérard combine comfort, country warmth and some of the best food in France. From their neatly kept gardens come the herbs and salad to accompany the local fish, shellfish and chicken that Michel grills over a huge open fireplace in the kitchen. Here is the place to sample the best of *cuisine minceur* or spa cuisine, as well as its *gourmande* counterpart.
Eugénie-les-Bains, Geaune, France
Tel: 58 05 06 07

ALISON PRICE
Alison Price is a graduate of the Cordon Bleu School. She enhanced her skills working with Pierre Koffmann at La Tante Claire and founded Alison Price Catering in 1981. Although equipped to handle a gala event of up to 4000, Alison values the smaller private dinner and cocktail parties where she and her staff can offer very personal attention coupled with a highly original approach to food.

Alison Price Catering,
5 The Talina Centre,
Bagleys Lane, London
Tel: (0171) 371 5133

WOLFGANG PUCK
Chef Wolfgang Puck is the Austrian-born and classically trained originator of the casual, lighthearted and theatrical "California Cuisine". His inspired and whimsical use of "designer salads and pizza" catapulted him to celebrity status after the opening of his landmark Hollywood restaurant, Spago. Now the creative force behind numerous restaurants and the author of several bestselling cookery books, Chef Puck remains the extremely popular spokesperson for fun, quality dining.
Spago, 1114 Horn Avenue,
West Hollywood, California, USA
Tel: (310) 652 4025

STEPHAN PYLES
Chef Stephan Pyles, a native Texan, is one of the most articulate and creative forces behind America's culinary movement towards complex combinations of pure and intense flavours. Unashamedly proud of the Lone Star State, he commissioned local craftsmen to realize a sophisticated "rustic Texan" ambience as a showcase for his celebrated cuisine at Dallas's Star Canyon Restaurant. Chef Pyles's *The New Texas Cuisine* is a mouthwatering record of his imaginative culinary explorations in search of satisfying, sophisticated and aggressively flavoured food.
Star Canyon, 3102 Oak Lawn Avenue, Suite 144, Dallas, Texas, USA
Tel: (214) 520 7827

RESTAURANT LA BAGATELLE, AT LE GRAND CHALET
Chef: Christophe Chastellain
Christophe Chastellain's apprenticeship was under the guidance of the renowned Frédy Girardet of Crissier. Following appointments at the Baur au Lac in Zürich, at Witzigmann in Munich and Comme Chez Soi in Brussels, the latter two holders of three Michelin stars, he now directs seven cooks at La Bagatelle, the excellent restaurant of the recently opened Le Grand Chalet Hotel in Gstaad.
Gstaad, Switzerland
Tel: (030) 832 52

RESTAURANT LE CHANTECLER, AT THE HOTEL NEGRESCO
Probably the only place to stay in Nice itself, the Hotel Negresco is a grand, gilded example of the belle époque in which it was built. The wonderful restaurant, Le Chantecler, serves magnificent cuisine, worthy of its setting.
37 Promenade des Anglais, Nice, France
Tel: 93 88 39 51

THE RIVER CAFÉ
Chefs/owners: Ruth Rogers and Rose Gray
This fashionable Thameside restaurant, designed by Sir Richard Rogers, is the brainchild of the chef/owners Ruth Rogers and Rose Gray. This, they say, is where the London renaissance in Italian cooking started and sophisticated locals love the new wave of dishes it swept in. The inventive menus use the best ingredients to produce the authentic

northern Italian taste. One should go if only for the olive oil and the heavenly puddings. Thames Wharf, Rainville Road, London
Tel: (0171) 381 8824

ROYAL AUTOMOBILE CLUB
Founded in 1897 for the "Protection, Encouragement and Development of Automobilism", the Royal Automobile Club in Pall Mall now has 13,500 full members and is probably the largest private gentlemen's club in Europe. Members have the use of a swimming pool, Turkish bath, squash courts, banqueting rooms and 73 bedrooms, as well as the two restaurants offering both French and English cuisine. Club members can also avail themselves of the two golf courses, sports facilities and function rooms at the country club in Epsom, Surrey.
89 Pall Mall, London
Tel: (0171) 930 2345

RULES
Not so much a restaurant, more a London legend, Rules has been serving customers since 1798. It has been a favourite with actors, opera singers and writers from Dickens to Graham Greene. Edward VII used to dine here in private with Lillie Langtry. The specialities served in its warren of rooms are beef and game (from Rules' own Pennine estate) plus pies and puddings and wonderful oysters.
35 Maiden Lane, London
Tel: (0171) 836 5314

ST QUENTIN RESTAURANT
Named after the famous food critic, Quentin Crewe, this restaurant is so authentically a slice of French nineteenth-century brasserie tradition that exiles from France often book a

table just to remind themselves of home. The service in the *belle époque* dining room, with its mirrors and gleaming brass, is by waiters in formal black and white. The food is in the grand Parisian style.
243 Brompton Road, London
Tel: (0171) 589 8005

SANTINI
Sister restaurant to Santini in Milan and L'Incontro, this stylish establishment on Ebury Street is also owned by Gino Santin. It's a favourite with theatre-goers, international visitors and celebrities, who enjoy a selection of Venetian dishes cooked to perfection and served at a smart pace.
29 Ebury Street, London
Tel: (0171) 730 4094

DELIA SMITH
Living in Suffolk, England, Delia Smith is Britain's most successful and democratic cookery writer. She is the modern-day Mrs Beeton and sales of her *Complete Cookery Course, Summer Collection* and others now top 5 million. She says that the greatest compliment she has been paid was by a housewife at a book signing who whispered, "What I love about you, Delia, is that your recipes always work, even for an idiot like me!"

LA TANTE CLAIRE
Chef/proprietor: Pierre Koffmann
In the world of haute cuisine, Pierre Koffmann, the chef/proprietor of this Chelsea restaurant, has achieved the highest accolade – three Michelin stars and a universal endorsement that his food would be worth walking over hot coals to enjoy. What's more, the restaurant itself is not

a heavyweight temple of gastronomy but is a light and sunny place with pastel pictures, pale wood and yellow chairs. A visit to La Tante Claire is a life-enhancing treat.
68 Royal Hospital Road, London
Tel: (0171) 352 6045

TERRY TAN
Food consultant and teacher of oriental cooking, Terry Tan is passionately interested in raising awareness of eastern cuisine. He used to work at the influential Memories of China cookery school owned by Ken Lo. His lessons these days are organized on a private basis. Mr Tan is also the Chief Editor of the international edition of *Wine and Dine*.
No. 4 Caudron, Little Strand, Colindale, London
Tel: (0181) 205 9959

THE THAI COOKING SCHOOL
Repeatedly voted "Best Hotel in the World", the Oriental in Bangkok is recognized for some of the finest dining in Asia. The Thai Cooking School, conducted in English for the hotel's guests, provides a unique opportunity to learn not just Thai cooking techniques but the history and origin of an ancient cuisine. Classes are held in a charming, nineteenth-century building that might have featured in a Somerset Maugham novel.
The Oriental, Bangkok, Thailand
Tel: 236 0400

LE TITI DE PARIS
Chef/owner: Pierre Pollin
This is a comfortably elegant restaurant located in Chicago's northwest suburb of Arlington Heights. Chef/owner Pierre Pollin, a native of Normandy, describes his cuisine as "innovative French". Creative

combinations of fresh ingredients, extensive use of fresh herbs and beautiful presentation are the hallmarks of this fine restaurant. Chef Pollin counts among his many awards the prestigious DiRoNa (Distinguished Restaurants of North America).
1015 West Dundee Road, Arlington Heights, Illinois, USA
Tel: (708) 506 0222

TRIBECA GRILL
This stylishly casual Manhattan hot spot is located off the beaten track in a luxuriously converted TriBeCa warehouse. This exciting yet comfortable restaurant regularly hosts a famous clientele including founding partner, Robert De Niro. The spacious bar/dining area, Skylight Room, Loft and private movie screening room have made this a prestigious location for star-studded private parties. The food is wholesome; grilled seafood and pastas with excellent salads are the house favourites.
375 Greenwich Street, New York City
Tel: (212) 941 3900

TURF CLUB
An aristocratic club which recently counted sixteen dukes among its members, the Turf Club was established in 1868. Most leading race-horse owners belong. The members often shoot, and therefore a great deal of pheasant, woodcock and grouse is served. In 1975, the club sold the freehold of its Piccadilly property and moved to its present address, a house once occupied by Lord Palmerston.
5 Carlton House Terrace, London
Tel: (0171) 930 8555

TURNBERRY HOTEL
For nearly a century Turnberry, which overlooks the famous links of Ailsa and Arran, has been one of Scotland's leading sporting hotels. It opened as the country's first golfing resort using its two magnificent 18-hole golf courses. The tradition continues today with Turnberry providing a full sporting pro-gramme including tennis and riding plus state-of-the-art spa and beauty facilities. Eating can be light at the spa or a fine blend of classic and modern cuisine in the main restaurant.
Turnberry Hotel, Ayrshire, Scotland KA26 9LT
Tel: (01655) 331000

VANDERBILT RACQUET CLUB
The "Ladies Who Lunch" at this private club know it as one of the best places for a delicious but healthy treat after a set or two of tennis. In fact, since the club has eighteen indoor courts, ten professional tennis coaches, a gym, aerobics classes and facilities for massage and beauty work, it is a place to spend the day – especially as the Vanderbilt is known as one of London's most sociable and friendly sporting clubs.
31 Sterne Street, London
Tel: (0181) 743 9822

VENICE SIMPLON-ORIENT-EXPRESS
The journey from London to Venice on the Orient Express is still one of Europe's most sump-tuous and glamorous pleasures. Recreated in all the elegant detail of the 1920s, the train is a wonderful reminder of pre-war luxury and service. The dining saloon is, of course, a central feature of the train and

its high standards put it in the same league as some of the world's best restaurants.
Sea Containers House, 20 Upper Ground, London
Tel: (0171) 928 6000

VENTICELLO RISTORANTE
Nestling between San Francisco's famous Nob and Russian hills, the Venticello Ristorante is renowned for its warm and welcoming Tuscan country-kitchen ambience and innovative Italian cuisine. Patrons delight in the wonderful aromas emanating from the central woodburning oven while enjoying classically inspired dishes that make use of only the freshest ingredients available. Chef David Bastide changes the menu weekly to highlight bountiful local ingredi-ents which sparkle to perfection under his sensitive touch.
1257 Taylor Street, San Francisco, California, USA
Tel: (415) 922 2545

CAROLINE WALDEGRAVE
Caroline Waldegrave says she can blame her career in cooking on illness. A bout of glandular fever when she was a teenager put her behind in academic work and she was "packed off" to a Cordon Bleu course instead of university. It turned out well because Caroline now owns and runs Leith's School of Food and Wine in London and has co-authored several successful cookery books. Demands on her time have made dinner parties at home something of a delicious rarity.

WELCOMBE HOTEL AND GOLF COURSE
From the Lady Caroline suite with its four-poster bed, draw-ing room and study, fortunate guests can look out over the parkland surrounding this hand-some Jacobean-style mansion. The grounds encompass an 18-hole golf course, Italian garden and a water garden. Visitors to Stratford-upon-Avon come here for the best of English comfort and cuisine.
Warwick Road, Stratford-upon-Avon, Warwickshire, England
Tel: (01789) 295252

WHITE'S
White's Club in St James's Street is a world-famous gentle-man's club. Founded in White's Chocolate House in the 1690s, its members tend to be the great, the good and the affluent. It was once known for its mad gambling – in a famous incident Lord Arlington put £3000 on a race of raindrops down a win-dowpane. Now, in more sober times, one of the chief pleasures of the club is its magnificent English food.
37–8 St James's Street, London
Tel: (0171) 493 6671

WINDSOR COURT HOTEL
The Windsor Court is the grandest and best hotel in New Orleans, located in the central business district, a short walk from the romantic French Quarter. The distinguished Grill Room proudly presents the celebrated Kevin Graham's inspired international cuisine in an elegant contemporary setting. Using his firm classical

training as a springboard, Chef Graham creates mouth-watering contemporary dishes which have gained him world-wide acclaim.
300 Gravier Street, New Orleans, Louisiana, USA
Tel: (504) 523 6000

OPRAH WINFREY
Oprah needs no introduction as the First Lady of American tele-vision. Her frank and open style has made her talk show and celebrity interviews popular with audiences around the world. Nothing if not versatile, Oprah has been a news anchorwoman, an actress and now takes the credit as one of the US's leading television executives.

YEW TREE INN
Chef: Michael Ferguson
Having cooked for years at some of London's most famous establishments, including Mirabelle's, Claridge's and Brown's Hotel, Chef Ferguson decided to take his unique brand of fine cooking, original recipes and delightful presenta-tion to his own pub and restau-rant in Hampshire. His gâteau of salmon is delicious, a delicate but fulfilling melt-in-the-mouth offering, worth travelling miles to savour. London's loss has been Hampshire's gain.
Lower Wield, near Arlesford, Hampshire, England
Tel: (01256) 389224

INDEX

....